YOUR KITTEN'S
FIRST YEAR

YOUR KITTEN'S

FIRST YEAR

DON HARPER

ILLUSTRATED BY JANICE NICOLSON

CHARTWELL
BOOKS, INC.

A QUINTET BOOK

Published by Chartwell Books A Division of
Book Sales, Inc.
114 Northfield Avenue
Edison, New Jersey 08837

ISBN 0-7858-0163-4

This book was designed and produced by
Quintet Publishing Limited
6 Blundell Street
London N7 9BH

Creative Director: Richard Dewing
Designer: James Lawrence
Project Editor: Anna Briffa
Illustrator: Janice Nicolson

Typeset in Great Britain by
Central Southern Typesetters, Eastbourne
Manufactured in Hong Kong by
Regent Publishing Services Ltd.
Printed in China by
Leefung-Asco Printers Ltd.

CONTENTS

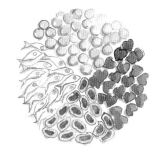

BEFORE YOU
DECIDE

———— ∞ ————

ABOVE: All cats are
inquisitive by nature.

Cats have a popular image as independent companions, especially when compared with dogs, but caring for a cat properly is still a daily responsibility. Acquiring a cat is not something that should be entered into lightly, because a cat can often live well into its teens, and the costs of caring for it over this period will not be insignificant.

Apart from feeding your pet, you will also have veterinary expenses and probably the cost of insurance, as well as cattery fees if you need to go away and leave your cat at any stage. You may not have to pay for a crossbred kitten, but there could alternatively be the additional burden of purchasing a pedigree kitten to be taken into consideration at the outset. You will have to be prepared to devote time to grooming a cat, on a daily basis if it is long-haired, as well as simply making a fuss of it. Should you not feel able to make this type of commitment, a cat of any age is not a suitable pet for you.

If you start out with a young kitten, there will be additional strains on the household. The cute, fluffy bundle of fur will almost inevitably cause some damage in your home soon after its arrival, scratching furniture or fabrics. It may soil indoors as well – a vice that is not restricted to young cats. Its hunting skills can result in wildlife, such as mice and birds, being brought indoors, if not dead, shocked, and injured and, even if you are squeamish about such matters, you will need to be prepared to intervene in this situation.

You will also have to consider other family members who may be affected by a cat in the home. Allergies to cats, causing symptoms similar to asthma, as well as repeated sneezing and runny eyes, are not uncommon. Research is being carried out to find a possible vaccine, but at present there is little that can be done to assist sufferers. As a result, susceptible individuals should not be exposed to close contact with a cat. Long-haired cats tend to provoke the worst reaction, and this may need to be considered when you are choosing a pet. If you have doubts whether a member of the family could be allergic, it may be better to start by fostering a cat for an animal welfare organization rather than commit yourself to take a cat on a permanent basis, only to discover that a family member has an allergic reaction. Then you will almost certainly need to find another home for the cat, which will be distressing for you and disorienting for it.

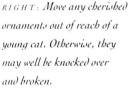

RIGHT: Move any cherished ornaments out of reach of a young cat. Otherwise, they may well be knocked over and broken.

YOUR SURROUNDINGS

One of the reasons that cats have grown so much in popularity as pets in recent years is their adaptable nature. Although it is desirable for cats to have outdoor access, it seems that they can live quite contentedly indoors on a permanent basis. They can, in consequence, be kept in apartments where it would be difficult, if not impossible, to accommodate a dog.

As worries over the number of cats being killed or injured on the streets of major towns and cities each year increase, more cat-owners are opting to house their pets indoors, allowing them outside only under supervision. This can entail extra costs, however, because you may need to invest in an outdoor run cattery, where your pet can be allowed to exercise regularly. Provided you have sufficient space in the

LEFT: It is possible to keep a cat indoors permanently, but you will need to adjust your home accordingly.

ABOVE: Grass kits are advisable for cats that are kept indoors on a permanent basis.

yard for this type of structure, this approach may also be recommended if a member of the family is allergic to cats. The cat can be housed safely, without harming the health of the allergy sufferer, although this is obviously not as ideal as having a cat that can live indoors for at least part of the time.

If your cat is to be kept indoors permanently, you will need to provide a suitable playing area – in the corner of a room, for example – and also items such as grass, which would probably be eaten by a free-roaming cat. Special seed kits are available from pet stores for this purpose, together with a range of climbing frames and playthings.

It is obviously important to provide every encouragement to a kitten that is settling into a new home. You should, for example, avoid obtaining your new pet and then having to go away soon afterward so that you have to put it in a cattery. This may have long-term

BELOW: Some rearrangements to your home may be necessary to protect ornaments and other valuables from being knocked over by your cat.

consequences, because studies suggest that the early days are critical in establishing a close bond between a cat and its owner.

Similarly, it is not a good idea to introduce a young kitten to the home when there are seasonal festivities such as Christmas, because you will be unlikely to be able to spend enough time with your new pet. Lack of supervision at this time may result in your not noticing the onset of illness or the kitten's getting into trouble – stealing food from the kitchen, for example. Other changes in domestic circumstances, such as the arrival of a new baby, may also mean that it will be better to wait for some months before obtaining a kitten.

You may face some opposition to the acquisition of a kitten from established pets. An older cat is unlikely to embrace a newcomer readily, although the reaction is hard to predict and will depend on the individuals concerned. The kitten may attempt to play with its older companion and is likely to be rebuffed, although in time they may strike up a bond together.

RIGHT: An older cat may not initially appreciate sharing its home with a new kitten but, in time, they may strike up a close bond.

A dog will need to be watched carefully when you acquire a kitten, because it may attempt to bully it at first. In time, though, the cat is likely to be dominant. Conflict is most likely to arise at feeding times, and for this reason the pets should be fed in separate rooms to avoid possible conflict.

Kittens can be especially demanding until they are settled into the home. It may, therefore, be a good idea to schedule part of your vacation allowance to coincide with the

CATS AND OWNERS

Older owners, who spend most of their time at home, are sometimes deterred from keeping a cat, particularly if they live alone. They often worry about what might happen if they found themselves unable to look after their cat in the future. There are now various organizations that will help to care for pets whose owners fall ill, and the positive health benefits of keeping a cat should, in any case, outweigh this worry. People who keep pets are generally more positive in their outlook, and noticeable physical benefits, such as lowered blood pressure, can follow from stroking a cat, helping owners as well as their pets to relax successfully. There are also very real benefits for children who grow up in a home with a cat. It will afford them an insight into the natural world and introduce them to the responsibility of caring for pets. They may also be attracted to showing cats, which can develop into a lifelong hobby.

ABOVE: Cats may rest in the most unlikely places, as here on the wheel of a car. Try to ensure that your pet is never in danger either indoors or outside.

acquisition of your new pet, so that you can spend time with it during the daytime, if you normally go out to work. A kitten is likely to require three meals daily, and it will benefit from constant companionship when it is first separated from its littermates and moved to a strange environment.

Keeping a cat when you are working elsewhere during the day is perfectly feasible, particularly because cats still retain the nocturnal instincts of their wild ancestor, the African wildcat (*Felis lybica*). This means that they will frequently sleep for much of the day, becoming more active in the late afternoon. Indeed, it is quite normal for cats to sleep for 16 hours every day and, after a period of play, a kitten will often be ready for a rest. It may in any event be possible to fit a suitable cat flap (see page 66), which will allow your cat to wander in and out of the home safely.

When it comes to feeding, you can offer fresh or canned food morning and evening, which will be sufficient for young cats, or leave dry food available for them throughout the day. If you will be unable to return home to feed your kitten at midday, you can invest in one of the automatic feeders that are now available. These will keep fresh food cold, even on a warm day, and open at a preset time, so that the kitten can feed itself.

You will need to supervise contact between your children and the new pet closely in the early days, while the kitten retains its novelty value, as it may be rather harassed by their constant attention. You will need to set aside periods when it will be allowed to sleep. You must teach your children to handle the kitten properly from the outset, so that they will not hurt it and it does not scratch them. When it comes to handling the kitten, you will need to ensure that the children know how to pick up the kitten safely, although it is probably not recommended that children under six years old be allowed to pick up the kitten. The children should also not be allowed to carry the young

LEFT: Playing regularly with your cat will help to develop the bond between you.

cat around. Instead, place the cat alongside of each child so that they can become acquainted with each other. Young children must be taught that cats are not toys and that they will feel pain if they are pinched or squeezed.

When children and cats play together the other aspect that needs to be considered is hygiene. Always make sure that the children wash their hands afterward and also before mealtimes, again under your supervision. This should largely eliminate any risks posed by the diseases toxoplasmosis and *visceral larval migrans,* which can be spread if children ingest the parasitic cysts or eggs.

You will also need to ensure that the kitten's litter box is placed as far out of the reach of younger children as possible. You may also need to make changes outdoors as well, especially if you have a sandbox for children, or the cat may start to use the sand as litter, and this can apply to other cats in the neighborhood as well.

The arrival of a baby can be a cause of concern to cat-owners, because of the cat's unerring ability to seek out warm places to sleep. It is a widely held fear that a cat may climb into a crib alongside of a young baby and suffocate it by sleeping over its face. The likelihood of this happening is extremely slim, but you should keep the bedroom door closed to exclude the cat – in any case, cats should never be encouraged to sleep in bedrooms. You can also buy a cat net to cover the crib or baby carriage as an extra precaution, to stop the cat from climbing in alongside of a sleeping baby.

There is absolutely no reason why there should be anything to fear about cat-ownership, and the pleasure of owning a pet cat is experienced by millions of people around the world. Caring for a cat is also now easier than ever, with a wide range of specially formulated, nutritionally balanced foods available to meet the requirements of a cat from kittenhood through to old age.

HOW TO HANDLE A CAT

RIGHT: It is important to handle kittens from an early age, so that they become used to it.

RIGHT: When picking up a kitten, always provide support for its rear end, so that it will be less likely to struggle or scratch you.

RIGHT: In due course, your kitten will relax when you lift it up, and will allow you to stroke its underparts, as shown here.

CHOOSING

A CAT

ABOVE: Don't rush your choice. You are looking for a companion who is likely to be part of your life for perhaps 15 years or more.

Most people prefer to start with a kitten when it comes to acquiring a cat. This has a number of advantages, including the fact that the young cat can grow up in a secure home. Older cats may have been mistreated earlier in their lives, and it can be difficult to win back their confidence. In addition, they may be more inclined to wander off to seek out their former haunts, especially if they used to live elsewhere in your neighborhood. Nevertheless, there are some drawbacks when it comes to starting out with a kitten.

The most significant of these is probably that a young cat will need to be fully housebroken, although this tends to be more straightforward than with a puppy, and it is now possible to obtain certain aids, such as sprays, to assist with the process. You are also likely to face additional veterinary costs with a kitten, not least for neutering, which is important both to make sure that a mature cat will live in relative harmony in the home environment, and also to prevent an increase in the number of unwanted kittens.

The cat's breeding cycle will mean that kittens are not available throughout the year. In the northern hemisphere, female cats will generally mate from the end of winter through to the following fall, with certain peaks occurring during this period, typically in the early spring and summer. The situation is similar in the southern hemisphere, with cats breeding at the equivalent time of year, from roughly October through to June. The falloff in day-length depresses the breeding cycle, and this may not occur if cats are housed indoors on a permanent basis. The environmental temperature appears to have little effect on the cat's reproductive cycle.

This temporary cessation of breeding means that early in the year in northern latitudes, kittens are less numerous than at other times. You are, therefore, likely to find a wider choice available from late spring through the summer months. This is probably also the best time to start with a kitten, as it will be more ready to venture outside when the weather is good, so facilitating housebreaking.

BELOW: Choosing from a litter of kittens such as these cute Somalis can be a difficult task.

ABOVE: Watch your kitten closely, because it could slip outdoors unnoticed, and end up in an unlikely, or even a dangerous, location.

PUREBRED OR CROSSBRED?

————∞————

You will need to decide at an early stage whether you want a purebred (pedigree) kitten, or a crossbred one. Although the differences between breeds of pedigree cats are less pronounced than they are in dogs, the breeds nevertheless do show noticeable variations in temperament. This aspect needs to be considered before you make a decision about which breed to choose. Do not be guided by the appearance of the breed alone, therefore, although such factors as the length of the cat's coat should not be ignored.

One particular coat color may appeal to you. The different colors, which range from white through shades of cream and red to blue (actually a grayish color) and black, are associated with a number of different breeds. More recent color introductions to traditional breeds such as the British and American Shorthairs are lilac and chocolate variants, and

the latter is particularly impressive.

Standards for all the different breeds and varieties are laid down by the authorities in different countries, and as a result, there may, be slight variations in appearance between members of the same breed. In the case of Burmese, for example, cats shown in North America tend to have a stockier appearance and shorter legs than their British counterparts. The breed standard lays down all the desired features of the individual breeds.

If you are interested in showing your kitten, it is vital that you are aware of the standard for the breed concerned and that you establish a clear idea in your mind of the features that judges will be seeking. This is not something that can be learned quickly. Before looking for a kitten, you should try to visit as many shows as possible and build up a picture of what is required. This will also give you an

LEFT: The patterning of bi-colored kittens will be consistent throughout their lives.

BELOW: Kittens and adult cats spend much of their time sleeping. This is not necessarily a sign of illness.

ABOVE: Crossbreeds are often easier to find than purebred kittens, and will prove just as affectionate.

RIGHT: Alertness is an important characteristic when it comes to assessing the health of a cat.

opportunity to note who is winning regularly, and obtaining a kitten from a successful exhibitor should help to make sure that you start with a cat of good appearance, or "type", as this is described in show circles.

It is, however, usually difficult to assess the likely show potential of a young kitten, because much will depend on its subsequent development. There will, of course, be cases in some breeds where the markings will be clearly flawed, ruining an individual's exhibition potential, but even in these instances, premature judgments can be misleading. Although the actual distribution of markings, such as the white areas forming the gloves in the Burman, for example, will not alter, many promising self (pure-colored) cats are born with tabby markings that are likely to disappear as the kittens grow older, so that these cats can be exhibited successfully once they mature.

Eye coloration is another feature that alters as a kitten grows older. At first, all kittens have blue eyes. These gradually start to change from three months onward, and it may be several years before the iris attains its maximum depth of coloration. This is an important consideration if you are thinking of acquiring a white cat, because of the link between blue eye coloration, white coats, and deafness. The cochlea, which receives the sound waves, is usually not functional for genetic reasons under these circumstances, and so the cat is deaf. It may, therefore, be worth deferring the acquisition of a white kitten until you can be certain of its eye coloration.

Alternatively, you may be able to obtain a response to sound from the cat. This needs to be carried out cautiously, however, so that the cat cannot use other senses to compensate for a lack of hearing. Do not clap your hands near the cat because it may see your hands or detect the air movement on its whiskers. The best way to find out whether a cat is deaf is to carry out the test some distance behind the cat when its attention is occupied elsewhere, at a mealtime for example. Deaf cats are clearly at a disadvantage when it comes to detecting the sounds of anything that may be of danger to them, and so, in urban areas especially, they are more likely to be run over if allowed to roam freely.

PERSIAN LONGHAIR

You may encounter three different combinations of eye color in the White Persian Longhair. There are the blue-eyed and orange-eyed variants, with the iris varying from deep orange to copper in the latter instance, and you may also come across the odd-eyed white, which has one blue eye and one orange eye. Such cats are usually deaf in the ear that corresponds to the blue eye.

A wide range of colors exists within the Persian Longhair category. These are all large cats, with round, massive faces and placid, affectionate natures. You will need to be prepared to wipe their faces regularly, as they sometimes suffer from tear-staining, because of the flattened shape of their faces, and food deposits may accumulate in the fur around their mouth. Regular, daily grooming is equally essential.

COLORPOINTED LONGHAIRS

The combination of Siamese patterning and the long-haired characteristics is reflected in the Colorpointed Longhairs, which are better known as Himalayans in North America. The so-called points – the face, ears, legs, feet, and tail – are darker in color than the body.

These Colorpoints have very similar requirements to the Longhairs as pets, but, as with Siamese and other so-called pointed varieties, you will need to take care if you have to bandage your pet. This is because the coloration of the fur is influenced by the cat's body temperature, which is normally lower at the extremities. If a leg, for example, is bandaged for any length of time, the hair there is likely to grow back paler, because the body heat will be trapped by the dressing. Similarly, if a pad is applied to the body, the hair will be darker in that area. For this reason, it is usual for females of the pointed breeds to be spayed (neutered), not through an incision on the flank, but from underneath, where the effects on the subsequent regrowth of fur will be less conspicuous.

BURMANS

Distinctive pointed markings are also a characteristic of the Burman, an ancient breed believed to have developed in Burma (Myanmar) centuries ago. In these cats, however, the pointed markings on the toes are replaced by the so-called white gloves. These white gloves are more extensive on the hind feet, extending up the back of the legs to the level of the hocks, and sometimes described as laces. It is difficult to breed kittens with the prerequisite patterning, but poorly marked individuals will nevertheless make excellent companions, being gentle and affectionate by nature.

SOMALIS

In some cases, you can choose from either long- or short-coated examples of basically the same breed – the Somali is the long-haired version of the Abyssinian, for example. These cats are being bred in an ever-increasing range of colors, although the Ruddy or Usual variety is the traditional form. They have "ticked" fur, with dark and light bands apparent on the individual hairs. Lilac, Silver and Blue are just some of the other colors now associated with these breeds. Extrovert by nature, Abyssinians and Somalis are also affectionate, home-loving cats.

TURKISH VANS

Another breed with a longish coat and distinctive markings is the Turkish Van. These cats are unusual in that they are the only breed that appears to actively like swimming. The breed originates from the southeast of Turkey, around the shores of Lake Van, which is an area where the temperature varies quite markedly through the year, with the summers often proving very hot, and the winters sometimes bitingly cold. These extremes of temperature are reflected in the cat's coat. In the spring, the cats shed much of their long fur, which then regrows during the fall. Their coloration is a distinctive shade of chalky-white, with restricted markings present on the head, ears, and tail.

MAINE COONS

Another breed that undergoes a fairly marked change in appearance depending on the season is the Maine Coon, a long-haired breed that has been evolved in North America. These are large cats, with males weighing as much as 18 lb. In the winter, when their fur is at its longest, a distinct ruff is evident around the neck. The Maine Coon has been bred in a range of colors, but bicolored forms are perhaps most numerous, along with individuals showing tabby markings.

A similar breed, the Norwegian Forest Cat, has been established for centuries in Scandinavia, and it is now becoming better known in other parts of the world. These are intelligent, hardy, and active cats, which thrive even in wet weather, with their coats having distinct water-repellent qualities.

ORIENTAL SHORTHAIRS

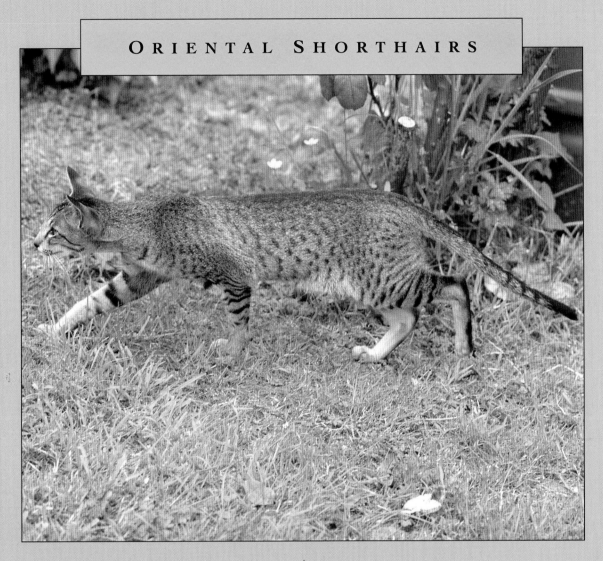

In recent years the traditional dominance of the Siamese among breeds of eastern ancestry has been challenged by the growing popularity of the Oriental Shorthairs. Blending characteristics of the Siamese with solid coloration, there is a huge range of varieties to choose from, which has helped to ensure their popularity. Interestingly, the blue-eyed white form, called the Foreign White, is unusual in that this cat is not generally afflicted by the deafness associated with other blue-eyed, pure white cats (see page 18).

In terms of character, both Siamese and Oriental Shorthairs tend to mature rapidly, and, when they are in season, queens can be particularly vocal. They positively demand affection and become very attached to their owners. These cats also tend to be athletic by nature, and they must have plenty of opportunity to exercise; otherwise they may set out to amuse themselves, by shredding the living-room curtains, for example.

SIAMESE

Still popular among the colors of the Siamese is the Seal Point, which is the traditional form of this breed, and which was first seen in Great Britain during the 1880s, having been imported from Siam (the country now better known as Thailand). The body coloration of these cats darkens as they grow older, forming less of a contrast with the points. The Blue and Chocolate Points are also widely kept, although the points of the Blue Point are slate-gray rather than blue. More recent introductions to the group include the Red Point, whose points are apricot-colored, as well as combinations such as Cream Tabby Points.

BURMESE

Distinguishable by its stockier profile, the Burmese is another, popular, short-haired breed, which, like the Siamese, is thought to have originated from Thailand, although these cats are perhaps more placid by nature. They are bred in a range of colors and combinations, such as the delicately colored Lilac Tortie, which has areas of both cream and lilac apparent in its coat.

The combination of Burmese and Siamese stock has given rise to the Tonkinese, which has intermediate characteristics, in terms of appearance, between these two breeds.

REX BREEDS

Best known for the actual texture of the coat, the rex breeds arose in the west of England, and they are named after the counties where they were first recorded.

The Cornish Rex, which has a distinctly wavy coat, is the oldest. This emerged in a litter of farm cats in Cornwall during the 1950s, and such cats were taken to the USA for the first time in 1957.

Publicity about the Cornish Rex led to the earliest reports of the Devon Rex in 1960. Although at first it was thought that they were the same mutation, it soon became clear that they are of separate origin. Both these rexes are available in a wide range of colors. It is important to note that the coat of young rexes is less profuse than that of adults. It may be 18 months before this feature develops.

BRITISH AND AMERICAN SHORTHAIRS

The nearest of today's pedigree cats to crossbreeds are the British and American Shorthairs, although both of them are considerably larger than the average crossbred cat. Male cats in particular develop prominent jowls as they mature, which adds to their impression of substance. Caring for these cats is quite straightforward, and they make very good pets.

You will also have a wide range of colors to choose from, including variants such as the Red Tipped, which you are unlikely to encounter in ordinary shorthairs. The fur of these cats is tipped, creating a reddish tinge, which contrasts with the white underfur. The underparts are also white. The Black Tipped, which used to be called the Chinchilla Shorthair, is another member of this group.

PUREBRED CATS

ABOVE: *This Siamese queen and her kittens are a beautiful example of a purebreed.*

There are over 50 distinctive breed categories of purebred cats. Some are scarce today, including the Manx, famous for its lack of a tail. In fact, in any litter of Manx kittens, there are some kittens with tails of various lengths, which is vital for the continuance of this breed.

The most unusual breed today is the Sphynx, which arose in Canada. Although it is sometimes described as the Hairless Cat, it does in fact have a variable amount of fur present at the extremities of the body, most notably on the tip of the tail. Other breeds include the Scottish Folds, which have flattened tips to their ears, and the recently bred Munchkin, with its dramatically shortened legs.

Less controversial breeds are continuing to be developed, such as the Burmilla, bred originally in Britain from crosses between Burmese and Chinchilla Longhairs. Spotted markings are also becoming fashionable, and new breeds, such as the Californian Spangled and the Bengal, have emerged. The Bengal, for example, is of hybrid origin, resulting from crosses between domestic cats and the small Asian leopard cat. Such rarities are correspondingly expensive, and demand from breeders frequently outstrips the availability of such cats.

You can track down breeders from the pages of specialist magazines or organizations, whose addresses are usually included in such publications. Most of the more established breeds have their breed clubs as well and, if you are hoping to exhibit your kitten and develop your interest in the breed, it will be a good idea to join the relevant organizations.

CROSSBRED CATS

Choosing a nonpedigree kitten should be relatively straightforward, and you will not have to travel too far afield, as may be necessary if you are seeking out a particular breed. Kittens in need of homes may be advertised in local newspapers or even in store windows. Alternatively, you can contact one of the animal refuges in your neighborhood, which will almost certainly have kittens in need of good homes, or will probably be able to pass you onto another group who might help you.

If you obtain a cat from a welfare organization you may be asked a number of questions about your lifestyle, and a member of the group may want to visit your home, to make sure that you can offer a permanent and suitable home to a kitten. You will also probably have to agree to have the kitten neutered when it is older, so that your cat does not add to the number of unwanted kittens in the future.

No one is certain of the number of homeless cats. In Great Britain the Cats Protection League estimates that about 200,000 are discarded for a variety of reasons by their owners every year. The figure in North America may be nearly 10 times higher. Without the work of voluntary groups concerned with the welfare of cats, the level of suffering would be much higher.

You should always give a donation to the organization when you take a kitten, to help it to continue with its work. You may even want to become involved as a volunteer worker yourself, either by helping directly with the cats or by raising funds for the group.

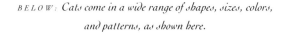

BELOW: Cats come in a wide range of shapes, sizes, colors, and patterns, as shown here.

GENDER

It may be hard to sex a young kitten, particularly if you are confronted with a single individual, but a careful inspection of the area under the tail should leave you in no doubt. Tomcats do not have an external penis, and so, superficially, there can be confusion. In adult male cats, however, the scrotum containing the testes is clearly apparent between the anus and the urethral opening below. The space separating these openings is much reduced in queens, and a similar difference can be seen in kittens, although the testes will be less apparent than in older cats. As a further guide, the opening of a female kitten tends to be slitlike, rather than circular, as in a male.

If you are seeking to exhibit your kitten and hope to breed cats in the future, it is probably best to start out with a young female. You will be able to select a suitable mate for her later on, when you will pay a stud fee, whereas if you have a single male cat, you will either have to acquire an unrelated female in due course or have to agree a shared litter arrangement with someone who has a suitable queen.

There is also the problem of coping with an intact (unneutered) tom around the home. Urine sprayed onto furniture and carpets will leave a lingering odor and, when a tomcat does venture outdoors, he is almost certain to

BELOW: Sexing kittens can be harder than sexing adult cats, but, in the female, (right) the openings are closer together than in the male (left).

become embroiled in fights with other male cats in the neighborhood. Abscesses following bites are a common result of such encounters, and a torn ear will inevitably ruin what may have been a promising show career. If you do have a male cat, therefore, it may be better to keep him in a suitable cattery with a run attached, if your ultimate aim is to use him for breeding purposes.

Some female cats can become very vocal when they are ready to mate, with Siamese being among the noisiest. You will also need to keep a close watch on them at this stage, because they will be keen to slip outdoors and find a partner. Cats are remarkably fecund animals. Their breeding cycle has evolved to maximize the likelihood of successful mating between solitary individuals in the wild, but, in

BELOW: Kittens that grow up together in the same home will prove to be great companions, and often avoid territorial problems in maturity.

domestic surroundings, cats are found at a much greater density than is the case for their wild relatives. An unneutered female, allowed to roam freely, will almost certainly end up pregnant within months, if not weeks.

Pedigree queens intended for breeding must, therefore, also be housed in a suitable cattery once they attain maturity. All others should be neutered, and this is a more costly operation in females, which may be a factor to bear in mind from the outset if you are simply seeking a pet cat. Males also tend to grow slightly larger than females, and develop jowls which are not seen in females. On the other hand, some people believe that female cats are more affectionate than males, and this may influence your choice.

If you are out for part of the day on a regular basis, you may be tempted to acquire two kittens, particularly if it is difficult to choose between them. You must consider the financial implications before taking this step, however, as it will double your expenditure. A cat on its own will not necessarily feel deprived of company, because, unlike dogs, they are not creatures with highly developed social instincts. Nevertheless, there is no doubt that it is better to start out with two kittens than to attempt to introduce a second cat at a later stage. Signs of jealousy and territorial dominance, often manifested by a breakdown in housebreaking, are often likely to be encountered. Kittens that grow up together will stay close companions throughout their lives together, sleeping and even feeding together, and they will rarely fight, since they are content to share their territory, although they may well hunt separately.

CHOOSING THE KITTEN

——— ∞ ———

If you are seeking a particular color or one of the rarer breeds, you may have to be patient and join a waiting list for kittens. The breeder will notify you when a kitten is available, and you will be able to arrange an appointment to decide whether you want it. If you see it before it is ready to go to a new home, which will be at three months old, you may be expected to pay a deposit.

Choosing an individual kitten is largely a matter of personal preference, although you may think that one individual is bolder or friendlier than another. You can ask the breeder to confirm your suspicions, because they will be in a better position to judge, having seen the kittens develop since birth.

Healthy kittens are bright and alert, with clear eyes and no signs of nasal discharge. They will walk without any evidence of lameness, and their coats should be bright, with no signs of lice or other parasites. Check the number of toes on each foot – some cats, particularly Siamese, may be born with extra digits, a condition known as polydactylism. There should be no sign of a kink in the tail, and the eyes should not squint.

A HEALTHY YOUNG KITTEN

TRANSPORTING YOUR CAT

———∞———

When you go to collect the kitten, you should take a suitable basket, rather than expecting the young kitten to travel on the lap of a friend. Most cats dislike traveling by car and may become disturbed as a consequence, particularly on a long journey. It is much better to place the kitten in a snug bed within a carrier in the hope that it will settle down and sleep for at least part of the journey.

A suitable carrier is, in any event, an essential part of the equipment you will need for your new pet and will greatly simplify

A SELECTION OF CAT CARRIERS

———∞———

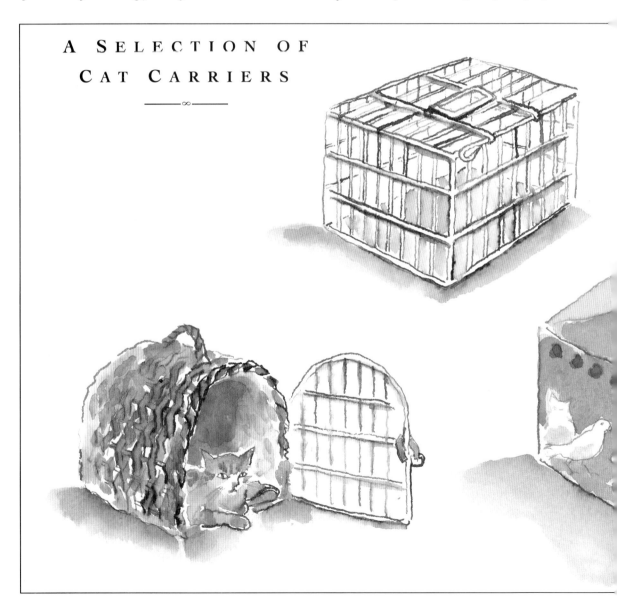

regular trips to the veterinarian or to a cattery.
A range of carriers can usually be found in pet
stores, but try to avoid those made of
cardboard. Although they are cheap, they are
not very durable or secure. If the kitten
empties its bladder on the way home, for
example, this will weaken the cardboard, and if
the bottom is not properly supported, the base
may fall apart, allowing the cat to escape,

which could have dire consequences. If you do need to rely on a cardboard carrier, make sure you provide additional strength for the base with thick packaging tape. Similarly, the top should be reinforced with string, so there is no likelihood that the kitten will be able to push its way out. The same applies in the case of an ordinary cardboard box and, in this case, you will also need to punch some ventilation holes around the sides before use.

The inside of the carrier should be lined with a thick layer of newspaper or absorbent paper toweling, with a suitable piece of bedding on top, where, hopefully, the kitten will settle down. Many kittens often miaow loudly, particularly when they are first placed in a carrier, but this should not be a cause for concern.

Wicker baskets, lined in a similar fashion, are a traditional means of transporting cats. Although it is less important with a kitten, it is better to start off with a basket that opens from the top, like a hamper, rather than one with a grille at the front. If a cat becomes frightened by being moved in a car, it will move to the back of the basket, spitting fiercely and lunging at your hand with its claws as you try to remove it. Lifting the lid, on the other hand, means that the cat will almost certainly try to slip out of its own accord, which will make it easier for you to restrain it.

One of the drawbacks of wicker baskets is the fact that they are not especially easy to clean, and they can start to smell if soiled. As a result, plastic carriers have become more popular recently. If you travel by other means than by car, particularly by plane in North America, for example, it is useful to have a carrier of this type, which conforms to the current International Air Transportation Association (IATA) guidelines for the carriage

CATS AND AIR TRAVEL

On occasions even young kittens are transported from one country to another. If you find yourself having to arrange this, you may find it easier to entrust the shipping process to a specialist company, which will organize the necessary bookings and advise you about current regulations, and matters such as quarantine and veterinary certification. If you are traveling home on a domestic flight, your kitten will probably not be able to travel with you in the passenger cabin, but try to arrange the bookings so that it will be on the same flight. This should help to eliminate problems that may arise if you need to make a connection to another flight. The risk of losing your cat as a result of a journey of this type is very slim, however, and airline procedures generally prove to be highly efficient. Whenever possible, try to avoid traveling when the weather *en route* is likely to be bad, to minimize the risk of problems.

of cats. You may again face some difficulty, however, because most of these carriers open at the front, rather than from above.

Show cats that have become accustomed to traveling from kittenhood soon take long journeys in their stride and do not get upset. It can be useful to take your cat out for regular drives in its carrier from an early age. Therefore, try to avoid doing this immediately after a meal, however, because the unfamiliar sensations of the vehicle may cause the cat to vomit.

You must be particularly careful on hot days to make sure that the cat is adequately screened from the sun. Never, ever, leave a cat in a car on its own under these circumstances, because the temperature within a vehicle can rise to a fatal level within a few minutes. It is possible to buy grilles that can be attached to car windows, which offer some ventilation when the vehicle is stationary, but these cannot be relied upon to protect your cat from the effects of heatstroke.

Never, under any circumstances whatsoever, should you transport a cat in the trunk of a car, in case gasoline fumes leak into this area. If you have a hatchback, probably the best option is to place the carrier in the rear of the vehicle, taking care that the air holes in the carrier are not likely to be blocked.

Within the car itself, try to avoid supporting the carrier on a seat. It is better to move the front seat forward and to place the carrier on the floor behind, particularly if you have floor trays in your vehicle. Then, should the kitten relieve itself on the way home, you can be sure that the urine will not seep onto the upholstery. In addition, the kitten is likely to be less upset by the unfamiliar sensations of traveling if the carrier is on a level base, and it will be secure there, if you have to brake in an emergency.

BELOW: Cat shows can entail a considerable amount of traveling for cat and owner alike, and kittens with a show career ahead of them will benefit from being accustomed to traveling from an early age.

WELCOME HOME

∞

ABOVE: Kittens will soon settle in a new environment.

You will need to buy a number of items of equipment before you bring the kitten home.

FOOD BOWLS

First, of course, food and water bowls will be required. Items of domestic china are not entirely satisfactory, although they can be used in an emergency. Saucers, for example, are less stable than specially designed drinking bowls, and you may find a puddle of milk on the floor if the kitten puts its foot on the edge of the saucer.

The traditional ceramic feeding bowls are sold in a variety of sizes by pet stores. These are ideal for either food or drink, because they are resistant to the kitten's teeth, impossible to tip over, and easy to clean. Stainless steel containers are lighter, but they may become badly scratched inside over a period of time. Plastic bowls are relatively cheap and designed for stability.

You may also be able to acquire a combined food and water container in one unit. They are available in various sizes, and a shallow-rimmed design is probably preferable, which should mean that the cat is less likely to end up with food on its face, which can be a particular problem with breeds such as the Persian Longhairs.

You will also need a small nylon-bristled brush to clean these bowls. Cats are quite fastidious feeders and may refuse food served to them in a dirty food bowl. It is not advisable to wash the cat's bowls alongside of your own plates for reasons of hygiene, particularly because cats have unpleasant bacteria present in their mouths.

You should use dishwashing liquid to remove traces of grease from the bowl, and the suds can be rinsed off under the tap. It is advisable to disinfect the cleaning-brush itself from time to time and it should be cleaned thoroughly on each occasion after use. Alternatively, you can use paper towels, and simply dispose of them. Even if you decide to offer your cat dry food, the food pot should be kept clean, although, in this case, it should also be dried with a piece of paper towel before being refilled.

BELOW: A selection of food and water bowls.

LITTER BOXES

The kitten will also require a litter box, where it can relieve itself, because at first it will be too young to go outdoors, particularly if it has not completed its initial course of inoculations. The kitten must, in any case, be kept inside for at least a fortnight, so that it comes to recognize its home territory and will be less likely to stray.

A wide variety of litter boxes is available, ranging from simple plastic trays to elaborate hooded cat toilets, incorporating an ionizer, which is said to overcome unpleasant odors. If you are intending to keep the kitten indoors on a permanent basis, it may be better to choose a more sophisticated design. In any case, however, it is useful to have a hood that can be fitted over the litter box, because this will help to prevent the cat from scattering litter around the room, as they usually tend to cover their feces.

A litter scoop may also be useful, as this means that it will not be necessary to discard all the litter each time that the box is used, but only the soiled area. In the interest of cleanliness, it is a good idea to line the base of the box with a piece of plastic sheeting. Then, when you do need to replace the litter, you simply have to lift out the litter on the plastic, which ensures that the base of the box remains relatively clean.

You can, of course, use garden soil in the litter box, but most people prefer to choose one of the specially formulated products sold through pet stores. Soil often contains small spiders and insects, which will not be welcome in the home, (it is also likely to stain the kitten's fur,) and its lack of absorbency means that the cat may acquire muddy paws.

The major drawback of cat litter is that it is relatively heavy to carry. This can create problems for older people, who may then have to purchase small quantities, which can work out considerably more expensive than buying a bulk pack. The range of litter material may vary from pelletized wood to granules of dry clay, often described as fuller's earth. Avoid using loose sawdust or shavings because these will stick to the cat's coat. Absorbency is clearly important, and, although some litter contains a deodorizer as well, this may actually not be appreciated by all kittens, and it may be worth changing the brand of litter if the kitten is reluctant to use its litter box, in case the kitten finds the smell of the litter distracting. Scent plays an important role in the life of cats, and the addition of a spray to signify the purpose of a litter box to a young kitten in new surroundings is to be recommended initially.

When you arrive home with the kitten, allow it to explore the home for a short period and then place it on the litter box. The first few days will be critical in ensuring that the kitten develops a routine of using the box, and siting it carefully in the home will facilitate this process. It must be readily accessible at all times, and it should also be in a relatively quiet part of the home, offering the kitten some security from children. The bathroom may be suitable for this purpose, although an outside porch or sunroom is perhaps better, because the kitten will be able to have free access. Ideally, choose part of the home where the floor can be easily cleaned and disinfected in case of accidents.

Most young kittens are likely to be housebroken by the time they are ready to go to a new home, and lapses are more often the fault of the owner, who fails to appreciate the needs of the young cat. If this happens, clean up the area thoroughly, to deter the kitten from returning to the spot. Repellent sprays are available for this purpose from pet stores, and, if possible, bleach should be used to disinfect the area.

A kitten is most likely to want to use its litter box after waking up or following a meal. It is a good idea to transfer it to the litter box at this stage and allow it to rejoin you in due course. If you find that a kitten persists in soiling in one place in the home, you may be able to deter it by placing its food bowl there, after cleaning the area thoroughly. Cats will rarely soil in the vicinity of their food.

Eventually, you will be able to persuade the kitten to relieve itself in the backyard, but you should still ensure that a litter box is available indoors as well. When the weather is bad or the ground is covered by snow, for example, a kitten may be reluctant to venture into the garden, preferring the security of its litter box.

Placing soiled litter on earth in the garden is often recommended as a means of encouraging a kitten to relieve itself there. You should, however, generally dispose of soiled litter in a refuse bag rather than simply tipping it onto a compost heap in the yard. This is because it may well contain infective stages in the life cycles of feline parasites, notably *Toxoplasma gondii* – the cause of the disease known as toxoplasmosis, which can be of particular concern to pregnant women – and *Toxocara cati* (see page 99). You should also wear gloves when you clean the litter box.

If you are using a pelletized wood type of litter, the best means of disposal will be to burn it if possible, as this will destroy any parasites. You may be able to flush clay-based litter down

a toilet, although this is potentially messy and can result in blockages within the pipes. Sealing the soiled litter in plastic bags should at least ensure that it is out of reach of other cats and represents no hazard to people.

The litter box will need to be washed thoroughly and disinfected at least once a week, with the contents being changed as necessary. A good layer of litter, at least 1 in deep, will encourage the kitten to use the box, so that any litter removed should be replaced with fresh litter, to ensure adequate coverage.

BELOW: A litter box and scoop, along with suitable cat litter, will be essential when you acquire a young kitten.

SLEEPING ARRANGEMENTS

Kittens will sleep for long periods each day, and you will need to consider purchasing a bed of some sort for your pet. Many owners prefer to choose a beanbag, rather than a conventional pet bed, and cats certainly seem to like the warmth associated with a beanbag, where they can either snuggle down or stretch out. It is important to choose a design that has a removable cover that can be washed easily, and it is sensible to insist on one with a fire-retardant filling.

If you prefer the idea of a more conventional bed, try to avoid those made of wickerwork, which will be much more difficult to clean than designs made of plastic. These can simply be washed and disinfected as necessary, ensuring that parasites such as fleas can be easily eliminated as well. A suitable cushion can be placed in the base as bedding. Washable pillows are recommended for this purpose – on hygienic grounds. The kitten will soon learn to recognize its bed, and will retire to sleep here readily, provided that it is positioned in a quiet spot, away from the main thoroughfare of the home. A corner of a room is an ideal place for the bed, provided that it is out of any drafts.

Training your kitten to sleep in its own bed can help to protect your furniture later, because it will be less inclined to jump onto sofas and chairs, digging in with its claws and pummeling the material before settling down to sleep.

BELOW: Snug sleeping quarters will provide a sense of security for a new kitten.

SCRATCHING-POSTS

———∞———

Scratching furniture is another problem that can arise as a kitten grows older, and, again, training at an early age should help to prevent this problem, which is particularly noticeable in cats that are kept permanently indoors. Indeed, it can become such a problem that owners may resort to having a cat's claws removed surgically by a vet. This operation, known as onychectomy, is banned in some countries, including Great Britain, because it is considered an unnecessary mutilation. A cat whose claws have been removed is definitely handicapped, being unable to climb successfully, for example.

Cats will regularly scratch tree trunks outdoors. This behavior not only helps to sharpen the claws, but also has a territorial function, serving to signify the cat's presence in the area to other cats in a visual sense, while scent glands located between the toes leave a further, olfactory, mark behind.

In the home, a cat will often accept a scratching-post as a substitute. Once the kitten is settled with you, it can be gently introduced to the post.

RIGHT: Cats will use a scratching-post readily. It can also serve as something to climb on.

Supporting its hindquarters, lift the kitten up slightly, so that its front legs are off the ground, and you can rub the paws down the scratching-post. In due course the kitten will learn to use the post by itself.

As a further inducement, you can dangle a catnip toy over the scratching-post, but within the kitten's reach. This should encourage it to start climbing up the post, as catnip is particularly attractive to most cats. Sometimes also called catmint (*Nepeta cataria*), especially in Great Britain, this herb contains a substance known as nepetalactone, which appears to attract cats. Kittens less than two months old are unlikely to respond to it, although the majority of adult cats find this plant attractive,

even in its dried state. The reasons for this are unclear, but it appears to have a certain hallucinogenic property, which appeals to cats of both sexes, inducing in them an apparent feeling of contentment. The only other plant known to induce a similar response is common valerian (*Valeriana officinalis*), the dried root proving most potent in this respect.

RIGHT: A huge range of toys is now marketed for kittens. Those scented with, or containing, dried catnip may be favored.

ENTERTAINING YOUR CAT

Kittens are naturally playful, and will appreciate a selection of toys. Although playing may appear to have a relaxing effect, it also allows a kitten to refine its hunting skills, which would be critical to its survival in the wild. There is evidence to show that a cat's ability to hunt successfully depends on its upbringing. Not surprisingly, farm cats prove far more effective hunters than Persians reared in catteries, although there are exceptions. Given the opportunity, most Siamese will climb trees and hunt birds almost instinctively.

Kittens will invent their own games with toys when they live on their own, although two young cats may prefer to play together for longer periods rather than accepting inanimate substitutes. Aside from toy mice, which may be leaped on and carried in the mouth, small balls are appreciated by many kittens. These can be pawed along the ground and chased, provided that they are light enough. You may also want to invest in a ball on a piece of rubber, which you can pull along the floor, inviting the kitten to jump on it. Even household objects such as an empty reel of cotton thread may be popular with your kitten. As they grow older, cats may lose some of their desire to play, but others may remain ready for a game throughout their lives, especially when encouraged by their owners.

Furniture for cats is now more widely available for those owners who prefer to keep their pets indoors on a permanent basis. The intelligent nature of cats means that they must have adequate mental stimulus when they are confined in this way; otherwise, there is probably an increased risk that a cat living on its own may develop behavioral problems stemming from boredom.

Climbing frames are popular with many cats, and they are produced for indoor surroundings in a variety of styles. Some kinds have hollow areas, so that the cat can climb both up the outside and also the inside of the frame. Again, toys may be hung off this type of equipment.

BELOW: Climbing frame and scratching-post, providing plenty of opportunity for cats to amuse themselves and to keep their claws in trim.

TAKING PRECAUTIONS

There are likely to be dangers in the home that you must bear in mind before you introduce a young kitten. Cats will sometimes nibble growing plants, and certain popular houseplants could prove harmful if consumed. These include Dieffenbachia, poinsettia (*Euphorbia pulcherrima*) and false Jerusalem cherry (*Solanum capiscastrum*), which has highly attractive orange-red berries that may fall onto the floor, where they may be leaped on and eaten by an unsuspecting kitten.

Try to assess the possible dangers in each room, so that you can take steps to minimize them as far as possible. If you have lapsed into the habit of not closing the door on a clothes dryer, for example, you will need to check carefully each time before filling and switching on the machine that the kitten is not asleep within it. The warmth in the barrel exerts a particular appeal over young cats.

Trailing electric cord can be a source of deadly fascination to young cats, and they may attempt to bite through a live cable, electrocuting themselves in the process. If you have the misfortune to find a kitten in this situation, it is vital to remember to switch off

BELOW: There are a number of hidden dangers in the home for a young kitten, including an open washing machine or drier, which could make a snug place to sleep.

the electricity supply and remove the plug from the outlet before you attempt to assist the kitten, otherwise, you, too, could be electrocuted. As a precaution, never leave appliances switched on with the cord in an accessible position while the kitten is left unsupervised in a room for any length of time.

In fact, it may be worthwhile acquiring a sectional wire-mesh pen, which can be clipped together and used to house the kitten securely; while the front door is open, for example. This will prevent the young cat from running out unexpectedly, possibly into the path of an oncoming vehicle.

A cat's jumping prowess can spell danger for it under certain circumstances, particularly within the confines of a kitchen. It is generally not recommended that a kitten be kept confined in a kitchen for any length of time, for it can prove to be the most dangerous room in the house. If you have built-in electric burners, the kitten could burn its paws severely, walking or leaping onto the hot surface. Similarly, it may spill a kettle of boiling water or a saucepan, scalding itself severely in the process while you are elsewhere in the home. Sharp knives left lying around represent a further hazard, as does tempting food – bacon being cooked under the broiler, for example. There are possible dangers at ground level as well. An iron, pulled off an ironing board by means of a dangling cord, could inflict a mortal injury on a young kitten.

Other rooms will be considerably safer, although you should not necessarily drop your guard, otherwise you could still find food disappearing unexpectedly off the dining-room table. Open fires will need to be covered with a secure screen, so that there is no danger that the kitten will be burned, should a smoldering log fall into the hearth, for example.

Some cats sleep so close to a fire that they end up singeing their fur. Although this creates an unpleasant burning smell in the room, it appears to cause the cat itself little distress. Hair, of course, is dead tissue, and so is not innervated – only if it is burned at the level of the skin will pain result. Move the cat away from the fire, however, because this can occur if it subsequently rolls over and actually touches the screen, particularly of a gas or electric fire, where the protective metal bars can be quite close to the flame itself.

Almost inevitably within the first weeks of acquiring a kitten you will assume that the worst has happened and that it has slipped out of the home unnoticed. This is where the choice of a name for a kitten is extremely important. Cats, like dogs, will soon come to recognize their names, and the naturally inquisitive nature of a kitten means that it will almost inevitably show itself when called by name, particularly if it is likely to be praised, or might receive a tidbit of food. You should repeat this process regularly indoors, as it will also be of value if your cat is to be allowed to venture further afield in due course.

Should you receive no response, it will be a matter of searching the rooms carefully one by one. It may well be that the kitten is asleep somewhere in another part of the home. Look carefully under dressers and similar items of furniture, and behind curtains. Kittens may also curl up under beds, even venturing under the covers in some cases. Less obvious places to search may be inside closets or drawers,

ABOVE: Kittens will want to explore their new environment. These young kittens are climbing the stairs. You may want to restrict their movements at times, using a sectional pen for this purpose.

where the young cat could be trapped, having crept in there previously to sleep.

A particular danger, if you are having any building work carried, out is a temporary gap in the floorboards. Many cats find the opportunity to explore below ground level irresistible, and they may venture here undetected, ending up trapped when the floorboards are replaced. The noise of the hammer frightens them, making them less likely to show themselves. You should always try to exclude a cat from a room in which the floorboards are raised, and never allow the boards to be fixed back in position until you are certain of the whereabouts of your cat.

Balconies can also be a source of danger, as can open windows if you live in a high-rise apartment block. Kittens in particular may lose their footing, after having been attracted there by a bird, for example, and then fall to the ground. Cats are actually well-equipped to survive this experience (see pages 61 to 63), and some are known to have fallen as much as 205 ft and lived, but, obviously, you must try to eliminate any risk of this type for, although the cat may well be able to walk away after a fall, it could have sustained a fractured jaw as the result of the impact with the ground. Doors leading to balconies should be kept closed as far as possible when the kitten is awake and in the adjoining room. Adult cats tend to have a greater sense of danger than kittens, whose mischievous natures can cause havoc on occasions.

FEEDING

In the early days your kitten may be having two or three meals each day, and it is always a good idea to obtain a diet sheet when you acquire your kitten and to use the food that it has been eating, for the first few weeks at least, to minimize the risk of any digestive upset.

When it comes to feeding cats there is a wide range of different foods to choose from, and their ready availability has done much to encourage cat ownership. Of course, there is nothing to stop you cooking fresh food for your cat if you prefer, but it will be harder to ensure that your pet is receiving a balanced diet.

Some cats can prove fussy eaters, and may starve themselves rather than sample a new food. Such preferences can develop in kittenhood, and so, once the kitten is settled with you, it is important to offer a range of foods.

RIGHT: Canned food is usually most popular with cats, because it has a high moisture content. Choose a complete, balanced food, however, containing all the necessary ingredients to keep your pet in good health. This should be clear from the labeling.

Cans are the traditional form of prepared cat food, but they are not without their drawbacks. First, they are bulky and a quantity may be difficult to carry, particularly if you do not have a car. Given a free choice, however, many cats prefer canned food because it approximates most closely to their natural diet, containing a relatively high percentage of water, around 80 percent in most brands. A cat will eat about two-thirds of

a 14 oz can daily, with kittens likely to consume slightly less.

Over the past few years pet-food manufacturers have sought to prepare different diets for the various stages in a cat's life, and you may, therefore, prefer to use a specially formulated kitten food, although the advantages of this over a regular canned diet are marginal. Kittens will appear to grow just as well on regular cat food, and they are certainly not at risk of developing any serious dietary deficiency if fed on a regular formulated diet.

The vast majority of canned cat foods available today are nutritionally balanced to keep a cat in good health and are supplemented with vitamins and minerals. They are typically flavored with items such as tuna, salmon, beef, and rabbit, but products of this type should not be confused with cans containing tuna alone. These have no supplementation and will not provide a balanced diet if used exclusively over a long period of time, although they can prove a tonic, encouraging a poorly kitten to regain its appetite, for example. If in doubt, check the type of food by looking at the labeling information.

Once they are opened, canned foods should be stored in a refrigerator. It is possible to purchase plastic can lids that fit over the open top to keep the contents free from contamination. Cats generally prefer warm food, and so it is advisable to remove the can from the refrigerator an hour before the meal, so that the food it contains will have an opportunity to warm up. Alternatively, pouring warm gravy over the food is likely to increase its palatability.

Fresh foods will deteriorate rapidly when out of the refrigerator, particularly during hot weather, when they are also likely to attract

RIGHT & BOTTOM RIGHT: Fresh foods can add variety to a cat's diet, but if used exclusively, they may result in nutritional problems.

flies. For this reason it is best to encourage your cat to eat all its food within a few minutes, rather than to pick from the bowl and return from time to time throughout the day.

Start as you mean to go on, leaving the food down for about 15 minutes and then removing it. Any leftover food can be stored in the fridge until the following meal. Your kitten should eat properly when it is trained on this basis, although older cats, which may be used to picking at dry foods, can be much more reluctant to adopt this style of eating.

It is always a good idea to use a fork to break up the canned food into smaller pieces. A kitten may have difficulty in breaking off chunks, and this can result in food being spilt and dragged over the floor. As a precaution, you may want to invest in a simple feeding mat, on which the bowl can be placed, so that any spills can be mopped up easily.

Again, it is important to choose a quiet place where the kitten can feed in peace. This will be especially significant in a house with other pets, particularly dogs, which will almost certainly attempt to steal the kitten's food. Placing the kitten in a pen while it feeds may be recommended. Try to avoid feeding it on a kitchen surface, as this will simply encourage it to jump up, and it could injure itself badly on a hot stove or something similar, as mentioned previously (see page 49).

There are distinct differences in the way that people feed their cats around the world. In Great Britain canned foods are still most

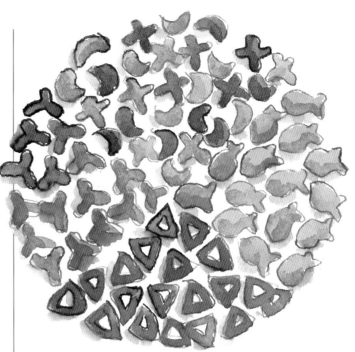

ABOVE: Dried foods will not deteriorate rapidly if kept dry.

popular, but in North America most cat owners prefer to use dried foods. The reason for this is partly historical, because, when dry foods were first introduced, they became the subject of bad publicity, particularly in Great Britain, where they were linked with the so-called Feline Urological Syndrome – often known simply as FUS.

Dry foods have a much lower water content than canned diets, and cats will not necessarily compensate for this reduction in their water intake by drinking more. As a result, there is a likelihood that the salts present in their urine will crystallize in the urinary tract and cause a blockage. This is the basis of FUS, although it must be emphasized that dry diets are certainly not the exclusive cause of this condition.

When the problem was identified, cat-food manufacturers altered the formulations of the food, lowering the level of magnesium. The blockage was actually caused by a magnesium compound called struvite and, today, the amount of magnesium present in dry foods is well below that contained in meat such as beef, as well as fish.

Male cats are more prone to FUS simply because their urethras, which carry urine from the bladder, are longer and narrower than those of females. Although FUS does still occur, it is now considered to be more likely the result of an infection of some sort than to have been triggered by the cat's diet. Dry foods now also contain more salt than was originally the case. This should encourage the cat to drink more fluid.

Kittens may be reluctant to try out dried food, especially if they have been weaned and reared on a canned diet. The lack of water appears to be the most significant deterrent in such cases, and you can overcome this problem by soaking a small quantity of dry food and offering it to the kitten. As a guide, simply cover the food with water and pour off the surplus once it swells; otherwise, the food may break down into a mash, which is not likely to appeal to the kitten. You can gradually reduce the amount of water added to the food at each meal, until you simply provide the dry food straight from the container. There are some distinct advantages to using a diet of this type, not the least being that it will help to keep the cat's teeth clean, preventing deposits of tartar, which can lead to dental decay and gum disease.

Bear in mind that, once it is wet, dry food deteriorates quite rapidly. In their dry state, however, foods of this type will not deteriorate if they are left out throughout the day, which can be useful if you are out for longer than usual. Leaving a supply of dry food will ensure that your kitten will not miss its evening meal if

you cannot get home at your regular time.

Dry food is also useful during the summer because it will not attract flies, unlike fresh or canned food. There is no advantage to refrigerating dry food – it can be stored in a cupboard – and it will take up far less space than cans of food. In fact, cats require only relatively small amounts of dry food, as it is a concentrated source of nutrients. As with canned food, the vitamins in dry food will deteriorate over a period of time, however, and it must be used by the recommended date shown on the container.

Fresh drinking water should always be readily available to kittens, particularly if they are being fed dried food. Place the water bowl near the food dish and make sure you change its contents daily. Stale water can be a breeding ground for bacteria, even though there may be no obvious signs of contamination. Every two or three days, wash the water bowl with a suitable detergent, rinse and refill. It can be difficult to keep a cat's fluid consumption in check once they are going outside regularly, because, in spite of your efforts to provide clean water, they may prefer to drink from puddles or garden ponds.

A third feeding option to consider for your cat is a diet based on semimoist prepared food. As their name suggests, these foods contain more water – around 30 per cent compared with the 10 per cent present in a dried diet – and are therefore more palatable. They tend to be shaped, to give an attractive impression, in the form of fish or even strands of mince. Semimoist foods come in small, sealed bags, and, once they have been opened, they should be kept airtight and used as soon as possible, otherwise the food will dry out.

If you decide to prepare fresh food for your kitten, it is important to bear in mind that cats are obligate carnivores, which means that they must have meat or fish in their diet if they are to thrive. Their wild ancestors lived on a diet of animal tissues, which are rich sources of protein and of fat. Cats require a higher level of protein in their diet than dogs, which is why cans of cat food are generally more expensive than those of dog food.

In addition, an essential component of protein, in the form of the amino acid taurine, must be present in a cat's diet, or its vision will be affected. Cats cannot, therefore, be fed satisfactorily on dog food, which is not supplemented with this vital ingredient, nor can they manufacture this amino acid in their body, like dogs.

If you want to feed mainly fresh food, variety is the key to keeping a kitten in good health, and it is worth remembering that price is no indication of nutritional value. The best cuts of steak, for example, are low in vitamin A, which is essential for healthy vision, as well as calcium, necessary for healthy bone development, and iodine, which is vital for the production of thyroid hormones that regulate the body's metabolism. Chicken is a relatively balanced source of nutrients, but you must make sure that there are no sharp bones that could become stuck in your kitten's throat. It is important to cook all fresh food, rather than

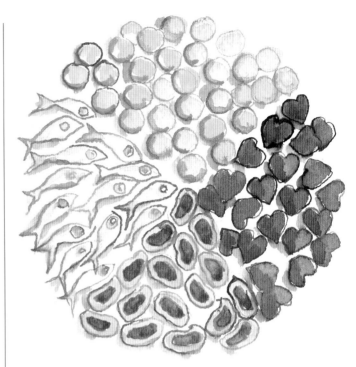

feeding it raw, because the meat may be contaminated by *Salmonella* and other bacteria, as well as parasites such as *Toxoplasma gonadii*.

Fish should also be cooked, because it may contain an enzyme known as thiaminase, which destroys vitamin B_1, and can lead to a deficiency. Cooking denatures this enzyme. Too much fatty fish – mackerel, for example – in a kitten's diet can be harmful, however, because it gives rise to the condition known as yellow fat disease or steatitis. A deficiency of vitamin E is likely to arise, which emphasizes the need to provide adequate variety when you rely on fresh food to feed your kitten.

There is little, if any, financial saving to be

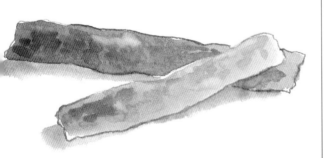

LEFT: Some cats will appreciate chews, which may help to clean their teeth.

ABOVE: Semimoist foods have a less crunchy texture than dry foods.

ABOVE: Some cats will nibble plants, and may also eat grass occasionally.

made from using a fresh, rather than a prepared, diet, especially as you will almost certainly have to use a vitamin and mineral supplement as well to compensate for any dietary shortcomings. Supplements of this type may be available from your vet, and it is a good idea to talk about the kind of diet that you are intending to offer the kitten at an early stage. You can then be advised on using such products.

Unfortunately, more problems are now being encountered with cats suffering from an excessive vitamin and mineral intake, because owners are tending to give too much in the form of supplements. Under normal circumstances, if you are offering your cat a balanced, prepared diet, then there will be little, if any, need to provide any additional supplementation.

If you do use a supplement make sure you follow the instructions for usage implicitly, so as not to place your kitten's health at risk. The effects of an overdose of the fat-soluble vitamins, which are stored in the body, can be devastating. A cat fed mainly on liver is at risk from an excess of vitamin A in any event, but the situation will be exacerbated by the addition of further vitamin A to the in the form of a general-purpose supplement. Stiffness and pain, notably in the forequarters, and deformation of the skeleton, are the likely results.

Many owners assume that it is vital for a kitten, or indeed an older cat, to be given milk to drink. Although many cats like milk and it is a valuable source of nutrients such as calcium, it is certainly not essential to their well-being, especially if they are receiving a balanced diet. In hot weather, milk will sour quite rapidly, and so only a small quantity should be given, immediately after a meal. The bowl should be washed out with a detergent, and rinsed ready for the next meal if you are using canned food or semimoist food. Milk should be provided in a separate bowl from dry food, and any surplus must be discarded before it can turn sour.

Not all cats are actually able to digest milk properly, and diarrhea may be the result, especially in Siamese cats and related breeds. This is because they lack the enzyme that is necessary to digest the milk sugar, lactose, which then ferments in the gut, often causing digestive upsets. It is, however, now possible to purchase special milk substitutes for cats. These contain low levels of lactose and so do not have this effect. The cartons, available from pet stores and supermarkets, need to be kept refrigerated after being opened, like ordinary milk.

Cats are not generally keen to consume vegetables, although they will often display a liking for grass. This may be either to supplement their diet with fiber or it can serve as a natural emetic, particularly if the cat may be suffering from a fur-ball or a buildup of intestinal worms. If your kitten is kept permanently indoors, you may find that it starts eating houseplants or even flowers, and this is clearly not to be recommended. You can acquire special grass kits for cats, which can be grown on the windowsill, and then placed on the ground for your pet once the shoots have developed. Cats tend to prefer relatively short, tender grass rather than coarse, dry stems. Eating grass need not be a cause for concern, although if you have not dewormed a young cat recently and it is proving a keen hunter (see page 99), this should serve as a timely reminder, particularly if the grass is subsequently vomited and worms are visible.

RIGHT: *If your cat lives indoors, you can still supply it with fresh grown grass. Special kits for this purpose are sold by pet shops.*

CARING FOR YOUR KITTEN

∞

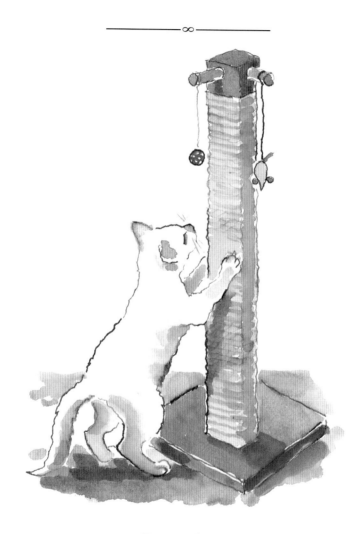

ABOVE: Watching is harmless, but, if your cat actually catches a bird, then try to persuade it to release its victim, firstly by calling the cat to you.

It is a good idea to arrange a veterinary checkup for your kitten after you acquire it. At the age of 12 weeks it will, in any case, be due for its second set of inoculations against cat flu. If you have not used a veterinarian in your area before, ask your friends if they can recommend someone. Alternatively, you can simply contact a practice through a listing in the telephone book. All veterinarians undergo rigorous training and will be well-equipped to care for your pet, and, although the larger practices tend to offer a more comprehensive range of services on site, you may prefer to stick to a practice where you are likely to see the same one each time you go.

You should have received a vaccination certificate when you acquired the kitten, and it will be helpful to take this to your veterinarian on your first visit. Some practices run an appointments system; others have set times, for example, between 10 and 12 a.m. This is something you will need to discover when you first contact the practice. If you are at all worried by your kitten, do mention it.

Assuming everything is fine, however, you should then consider insuring your pet against the costs of veterinary treatment for illness and accident. Kittens are perhaps most likely to encounter problems, particularly once they start wandering alone out of doors, and if your cat is unfortunate enough to be involved in an accident, you could be left facing a large and unexpected bill for delicate and skilled orthopedic work. Policies may also have other benefits, including some payment of advertising costs if your kitten strays.

LEFT: A harness and leash will enable you to exercise your cat in safety without it being able to run off.

Once the kitten has received its second set of inoculations, it can be allowed outdoors for the first time a few days later, but do not force it out of the home. If you have a back gate through which the kitten could escape from the yard, you should block this off with a piece of board at first. Keep a close watch on your kitten in the yard, and stay with it for as long as possible. You can keep its attention by playing a game using a ball perhaps, and finally call it back inside for a meal. In the early days, the young cat will be unlikely to stray very far.

It is also possible to train a cat to walk successfully, like a small dog on a collar and harness. Some owners actually exercise their cats in the street like this, although there are obvious hazards, such as passing dogs, which may frighten your pet. It can then become difficult to control your cat, because you are likely to be scratched should you then attempt to pick it up.

It may be helpful to obtain a collar for your kitten, which it can wear outside. This is particularly important if your cat shows strong hunting tendencies, as you can then attach a bell to the collar, which may help to warn birds of the cat's presence. It is vital to choose only an elasticated collar for this purpose so that the cat can wriggle free if it becomes caught up; otherwise there is a possibility that the cat could be strangled. This is one reason why flea collars are not always to be recommended for cats.

Apart from relying on a bell, there is little else that you can do to prevent your cat stalking and sometimes killing wildlife, and even a bell may not be very effective for long. Cats learn to move in such a way that the ball in the bell remains quiet, sounding only when they pounce on their quarry.

Cats are not instinctively equipped to kill their prey. This is something which they tend to learn from their mother's example, and domestic cats in particular may never have seen a kill, although they usually retain a desire to hunt. You may occasionally be able to rescue casualties alive from them. In the case of birds especially, keep handling to a minimum because of the additional stress this imposes, and seek veterinary advice about suitable treatment. Alternatively, you may have a wild-bird hospital in your area which may be able to assist and may be able to release the bird back into the wild. Sadly, although the bite may not have been severe, the bacteria introduced into the bird's tissues by the cat's teeth can multiply and prove fatal, which is why antibiotics are often vital in dealing with even minor injuries of this type.

Cats use their claws to climb a tree headfirst, but usually have to come down backward. In spite of the widely held belief that cats become stuck up trees, this is rarely the case. If left to

their own devices, they will generally come down in due course without need of any assistance. As they approach the ground, they usually swivel around and jump, landing on their forefeet. If they lose their balance at a greater height, which can sometimes happen, especially with young cats, they will instinctively swivel their body around in order to land safely on their feet.

*RIGHT. (above & below):
An elasticated collar, with a
bell attached, may help to
protect local wildlife should
your cat prove to be a keen
hunter.*

The main danger facing a cat outdoors today is traffic. Cats may be drawn to the street, sleeping under a car or stalking birds, and using a car as cover. Cats don't understand danger on the streets, and, even after being hit once by a vehicle, a cat is unlikely to stay away. They are at a particular disadvantage at night. Their eyes are adapted for nighttime vision, with the retina, located at the back of the eye, being packed predominantly with rods which function most effectively under conditions of low light intensity. There is also a reflective layer, the *tapetum lucidum*, behind the retina, which directs light back to this part of the eye where the image is formed. If a cat is caught in the glare of headlights, it will be temporarily blinded and so is less likely to be able to escape from the path of an oncoming vehicle. The unfortunate driver may see the light being reflected back from the cat's eyes, which glow in the dark because of the *tapetum lucidum*.

All cats, especially kittens, should be encouraged to spend the night indoors. Apart from the risk of death or injury from traffic, they are also vulnerable to nocturnal predators, such as foxes, which have penetrated into the heart of many major cities, and although full-grown cats do not often fall victim to foxes, young kittens are far more vulnerable.

If your cat is reluctant to come indoors at night, it will be helpful to develop a routine, whereby it is allowed out during the early evening and then encouraged to return home for its evening meal. Hopefully, it will then curl up and sleep through the night.

AVOIDING A FATAL FALL

RIGHT. (top to bottom): Cats possess a remarkable sense of balance, which enables them to swivel their body if they fall, so they will invariably land on their feet. These act as shock absorbers, helping to protect the cat from serious injury.

RIGHT: Tattoos have been used to mark cats, but these can become blurred over a period of time. Today, a microchip inserted in the cat's body by your vet gives lifelong identification, as it can be checked when required by a special reader.

EMERGENCY FIRST AID

RIGHT: A cat which has been run over is likely to be in shock. Seek veterinary advice without delay, to assess the state and severity of its injuries.

RIGHT: If possible, wrap the cat in a blanket or old towel, so that it will be easier to restrain, with its claws out of the way.

RIGHT: If the cat is bleeding badly, place a dressing of some sort on the wound and press here to stem the blood flow. A bandage can then be applied.

LEFT: Never tip a cat which is lying on its side after an accident. This could worsen any internal injuries, such as a ruptured diaphragm.

CAT FLAPS

———— ∞ ————

As your kitten grows older, you may want to allow it to move in and out of the home more freely. This can be accomplished by fitting a cat flap to an outer door, usually at the rear of the property and leading into the yard. There are various designs to choose from, some being more sophisticated than others. Some will swing in either direction, allowing the cat to push its way in or out, while others rely on the cat opening the door with its paw and squeezing through the gap.

Most young cats learn how to use a cat flap very rapidly, although, at first, you may want to leave the flap ajar and rely on the cat's

BELOW: Cat flaps are available in various designs. Left: this is a two-way door. Right: A basic cat flap. Cats soon master using a cat flap without difficulty.

natural curiosity to guide it through the opening. Some cats master the use of flaps without any difficulty, especially if there is food available within, and you may be unlucky enough to discover that you are soon hosting a gathering of the neighborhood cats in your kitchen. This can become a problem if the local tom decides to spray around the room, leaving a pungent reminder of his presence. For this reason you may decide to invest in one of the more expensive designs of cat flap, customized to admit only your cat. This is usually achieved by means of a magnetic system, with a magnet attached to the cat's collar, serving to unlock the flap once the cat is within range.

BELOW: An individual cat flap, operated by a magnet on the cat's collar to keep out unwanted companions.

BELOW: Security is important with cat flaps, to prevent unwanted intrusions by other cats in the neighborhood. This design is lockable.

ESTABLISHING A TERRITORY

ABOVE: Cats will occasionally fight, but, in most cases, the encounter is relatively brief, with the vanquished cat retreating fast.

In time your kitten will establish itself within your back yard, and it is also likely to wander further afield. Intact tomcats tend to establish the largest territories and will fight to maintain them, and for this reason alone you may need to have your kitten neutered in due course.

Cats living in towns evolve a fairly complex means of communication among themselves to avoid regular meetings in situations where conflicts might follow. They cross each other's territories on specific paths, which could not be seen as a challenge, and they often show a regular pattern of movements through the day. One cat occupies an area in the morning, for example, and its place is taken by another in the afternoon. In this way, peaceful coexistence is generally possible. Some cats do seem to take an almost instinctive dislike to each other, however, and are likely to fight whenever they come into close contact with each other, neither cat being prepared to back down. Fighting is only a last resort, and cats will, in general, try to avoid combat, with the weaker individual simply retreating.

When a fight does occur, it can prove a rather savage affair, being accompanied by a series of intimidatory howls and other calls. The best way to break up a conflict of this type is to throw a bucket of water in the direction of the participants. Unfortunately, their combat is

*ABOVE: Rubbing the head on branches will leave traces of
scent, and this serves as another territorial marker.*

likely to be renewed on the next occasion they encounter each other.

Apart from some loss of hair and possibly an injured ear, most cats will appear relatively unaffected after a fight. However, once the cat has calmed down, look closely for any flattened areas of fur beneath which the skin is visible, typically in the head and neck areas. Here you may see puncture marks resulting from a bite. If you bathe the bite carefully with salt water at this stage, you may be able to prevent it from developing into an abscess several days later, particularly if you apply an

RIGHT: After a fight, the puncture wounds under the skin left by a cat's sharp canine teeth can be a focus for an infection. A large abscess may form here. Regular bathing and antibiotics are then likely to be needed by way of treatment.

antiseptic cream as well afterward. The other cat's teeth will have introduced bacteria into the wound, and these are likely to set up a localized infection. The abscess will start as a small lump, and then swell up rapidly, almost to the size of an orange, becoming hot to the touch. Bathing with warm salt water will bring the abscess to a head, while antibiotics will help to control the infection. It is not uncommon for a cat to run a temperature and lose its appetite at this stage, but, once the abscess has burst, the cat should soon recover uneventfully.

GIVING A BRAN BATH

ABOVE: Bran can be purchased from pet stores for this purpose, along with the grooming equipment.

ABOVE: Rub the warm bran into the cat's coat. Leave it here for several minutes to absorb the grease.

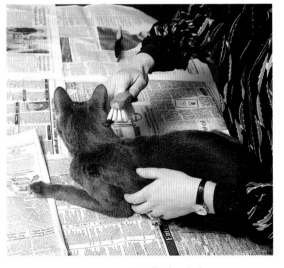

ABOVE: Finally, brush the bran out of the coat thoroughly, using a brush with natural bristles.

There will be occasions when it will be necessary to bathe your cat, particularly before a show, in which kittens can often be entered. There may even be a section for nonpedigree cats and kittens, which are judged on their condition and appeal.

Many cat breeders prefer to give a bran bath, rather than wet their cat's coat with water, which, when used with a shampoo, tends to create a fairly flat appearance once the fur has dried. To be honest, however, a bran bath is not as effective, although it will remove excess grease from the coat. The bran, which is available in pet stores, should be heated in the oven and then rubbed into the cat's coat, against the lie of the fur. Stand the cat on layers of open newspapers, preferably on a table outdoors, because this is a messy process. After rubbing the bran into the fur, you should brush it out thoroughly and groom the coat. A brush with natural bristles is recommended, because it will help to reduce the static, which will cause the hairs to stand up.

There may be occasions when bathing your kitten is unavoidable, particularly if it develops a bad infestation of fleas. In this case, you will need to use a medicated shampoo, as recommended by your vet, but, for general washing purposes, a mild children's shampoo can be used.

Most cats dislike water and should not be placed in a deep bathtub where they are likely to struggle. A plastic baby-bathtub is a much better choice, and this should be placed outdoors, so that water will not be splashed around the house. Fill it with tepid water and make sure you have a plastic cup close by to use as a bailer. It is advisable to wear disposable gloves if you are washing the cat with a medicated shampoo, especially if you have sensitive skin, and wearing a long-sleeved sweater or coat should help to protect you from being scratched if the cat resents its bath.

Place the cat carefully in the tub and, if possible, have someone else to hold it while you concentrate on washing it. Start by tipping water over the flanks and hindquarters, rubbing in the shampoo. Wash the head last, taking care to avoid the ears and eyes, and rinse off as much shampoo as possible before changing the water. At this point, wrap the cat firmly in an old towel and lift it out of the bathtub. Then rinse it again in clean water.

When it comes to drying the cat, make sure you bring it indoors. Then, even if it does slip off, it will be unlikely to catch a chill, whereas outdoors, deprived of the natural insulation in the fur, it could become cold quite easily. Many cats dislike the noise of a hair dryer and the jets of warm air anywhere near their head, so it may be best to dry the cat as much as possible with a towel, and let it complete the drying process lying in front of the fire. If you have a kitten, especially if you intend to exhibit it later on, it may be worth introducing it to the sensations of a hair dryer at an early stage in life, so that it will come to accept it without any problems in due course.

G R O O M I N G   A   S H O R T - H A I R E D   C A T

LEFT: Combs of this type are useful for removing dead hair from the coat, and prevent the formation of any knots.

Regular daily grooming of long-haired cats is essential to prevent their fur from becoming matted. There is also the risk, particularly when they are molting, that loose hair in the coat will cause fur-balls. These form as a result of the cat's own grooming activities. The surface of the tongue is rough, and the papillae will pull out loose hair as the cat licks itself. The hairs are swallowed, and are likely to coalesce in the cat's stomach, forming a fur-ball. These can become large, forming a blockage, which causes the cat discomfort.

The eating habits of a cat with a fur-ball are likely to change, and, instead of consuming its

RIGHT: Using a rubber brush. This can tone up the underlying skin as well as the coat.

LEFT: It is important to remove dead hairs from the cat's coat with a comb. Otherwise these may be swallowed and give rise to a fur-ball in the stomach.

RIGHT: Talcum powder can be useful to separate the hairs, if carefully sprinkled into the coat, but will need to be brushed out as grooming proceeds.

GROOMING A LONG-HAIRED CAT

RIGHT: Cotton balls can be used to clean around the eyes. Tear-staining can be a particular problem in some longhairs, marking the coat at the inner corner of the eyes.

LEFT: Brushing will give a good finish to the coat, and will also remove any loose hairs.

BELOW: Rubbing the cat's coat with chamois after combing and brushing can help to give it a good gloss, particularly in the case of short-haired breeds.

food at a single sitting, it will persistently pick at its meal. Although it feels hungry, the obstruction in its stomach will make it unable to eat its regular amount of food. If you suspect that it could be suffering from an obstruction of this type, you should arrange for the cat to be examined by your vet. In many cases, administering a laxative such as liquid paraffin – approximately 1 teaspoonful – either directly into the cat's mouth or on its food, should

overcome the blockage, but, in severe cases, surgery may be required.

You will be able to obtain a variety of grooming equipment from your local pet store, but other items, such as cotton buds, will probably have to be purchased at a pharmacist. Cotton buds are useful for cleaning the outer part of a cat's ears, but they should not be poked down inside the ear canal. If you suspect an obstruction or irritation here, contact your veterinarian for advice.

If the cat's fur appears to be tangled, using a wide-toothed comb should help to alleviate the problem. In severe cases, there may be no option but to cut out knots, because grooming will become too painful for the cat. Blunt-ended scissors are recommended under these circumstances, since, even if the cat struggles, they will not cause injury.

PERSIANS

Persians, with their relatively flattened faces, are particularly prone to tear-staining, because of the alteration to their naso-lacrimal ducts. The deposits, which run down the fur at the corner of the eyes, need to be wiped away with damp cotton balls.

A GROOMING KIT

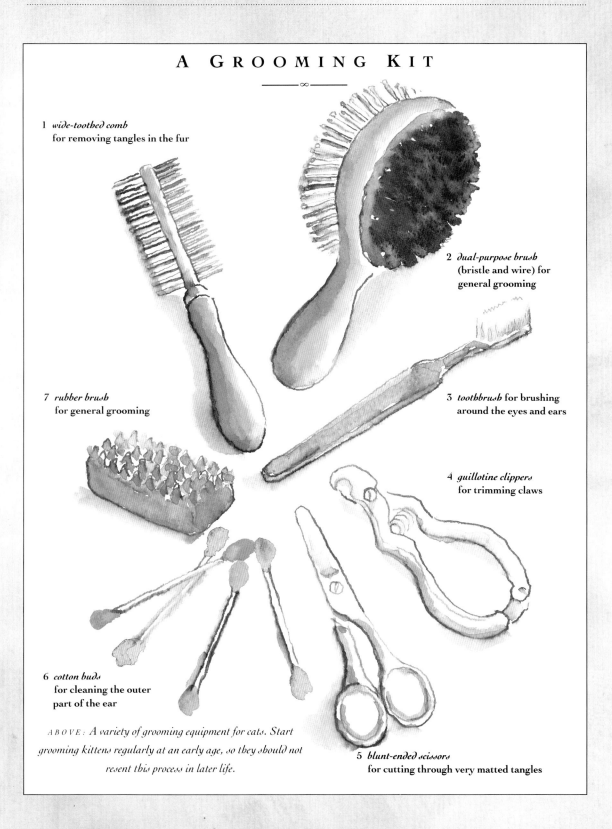

1 *wide-toothed comb*
for removing tangles in the fur

2 *dual-purpose brush*
(bristle and wire) for
general grooming

7 *rubber brush*
for general grooming

3 *toothbrush* for brushing
around the eyes and ears

4 *guillotine clippers*
for trimming claws

6 *cotton buds*
for cleaning the outer
part of the ear

ABOVE: A variety of grooming equipment for cats. Start
grooming kittens regularly at an early age, so they should not
resent this process in later life.

5 *blunt-ended scissors*
for cutting through very matted tangles

If cats are housed permanently indoors, it may be necessary to trim their claws from time to time. A pair of special guillotine clippers is ideal for this purpose, since the blade will not cause the claw to split, (the use of scissors may do so). Make sure you locate the blood supply to each claw before cutting – the blood vessels should be apparent as a thin, red streak extending a variable distance down the claws.

Cut beyond the point where this disappears – otherwise the claws will bleed – and remove any hooked ends.

Although kittens tend to have less profuse coats than adult cats, it is a good idea to accustom them to the sensation of regular grooming from an early age. Similarly, you should encourage them to allow you to pick up their feet, and to examine their claws.

CLIPPING A CAT'S CLAWS

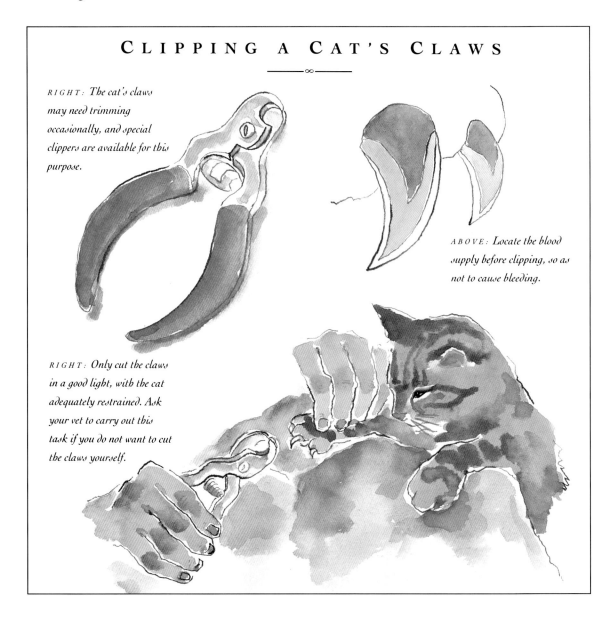

RIGHT: The cat's claws may need trimming occasionally, and special clippers are available for this purpose.

ABOVE: Locate the blood supply before clipping, so as not to cause bleeding.

RIGHT: Only cut the claws in a good light, with the cat adequately restrained. Ask your vet to carry out this task if you do not want to cut the claws yourself.

FROM
KITTEN
TO CAT

—∞—

ABOVE: Some cats are mature by six months of age.

The age at which cats attain maturity depends to some extent on the breed concerned. As a rule, long-haired cats are relatively slow to mature – the process may take 10 months or so in the case of Persian Longhairs. In contrast, other breeds, notably Siamese, mature rapidly, and may breed when only six months old. Females of all breeds tend to mature earlier than males.

You are most likely to observe a change in your kitten's behavior as it matures, with queens becoming more affectionate and restless during the pro-estrus period. This should be a warning to keep the cat indoors, because, if mating occurs during the subsequent estrus phase, you are likely to be presented with an unwanted litter of kittens.

Female cats also become more vocal at this stage, howling loudly to attract a mate, and almost sounding as though they are in pain on occasion. This may carry on for some time. Although the estrus phase should generally cease after about a fortnight, it may continue for months in some cases. Cats are unusual in a reproductive sense, displaying a phenomenon known as induced ovulation. Instead of the eggs being released from the ovary at a set time, ovulation occurs as the result of mating;

this increases the likelihood of kittens, because the eggs are always released at the optimal time for fertilization.

It is not normally recommended that a female cat in estrus be spayed (neutered), and in order to cause a cessation of reproductive behavior your vet will be able to trigger ovulation by artificial means. The cat will need to be kept indoors for perhaps a week or so, because repeated matings are not unknown, and she could still end up pregnant while there are viable ova within her reproductive tract. You should then arrange for her to be spayed before she starts calling again.

A calling cat can pose particular problems within a household, in particular because she will endeavor to slip out and find a mate. Neutering will mean an end to these difficulties and ensure there is no risk of subsequent pregnancy. There will be no other impact on the cat's personality, however, and, unlike dogs, cats generally do not put on weight after neutering, although this is something that may need to be watched.

Male cats can become equally troublesome in the home once they reach maturity, frequently spraying urine and becoming

RIGHT: Male cats in particular will spray urine as a territorial marker. Neutering will prevent this unpleasant behaviour.

involved in fights with other toms in the neighborhood. They may also disappear for days, roaming far afield in search of females. Neutering will help to overcome these problems, although the physical change which leads to the development of jowls will not be reversed by neutering. Normally, toms are neutered outside the breeding period, but this is not essential. A shortage of the male hormone, testosterone, may sometimes follow, resulting in some hair loss, but hormonal replacement therapy will compensate for this.

You are likely to find that your cat will have a longer life expectancy if it is neutered early in life. The surgery itself is quite straightforward, particularly for the male, and recovery is fast, although it will take a number of weeks for the fur to regrow on the female's abdomen where the incision was made.

NEUTERING

———∞———

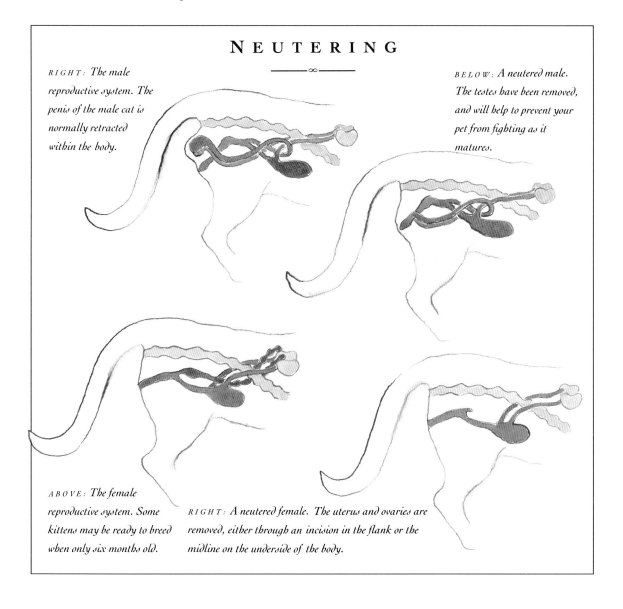

RIGHT: The male reproductive system. The penis of the male cat is normally retracted within the body.

BELOW: A neutered male. The testes have been removed, and will help to prevent your pet from fighting as it matures.

ABOVE: The female reproductive system. Some kittens may be ready to breed when only six months old.

RIGHT: A neutered female. The uterus and ovaries are removed, either through an incision in the flank or the midline on the underside of the body.

BREEDING CYCLE AND MATING

ABOVE: When she is becoming ready to mate, the female cat will call and become more playful, once she has attracted a potential mate.

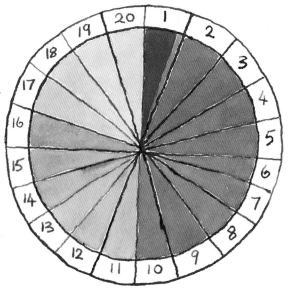

LEFT: A diagram showing stages in the reproductive cycle of a cat, measured in weeks.

ABOVE: *She will then crouch down, in a characteristic stance called lordosis.*

BELOW: *Afterward, the cats will go their separate ways, and the female will give birth and rear the kittens on her own.*

SEASONAL CONSIDERATIONS

ABOVE: A cat will often drink from a pond in the summer. Take precautions in the winter to prevent the cat from having an accident, should the pond freeze over.

As the year proceeds your young cat is likely to encounter unfamiliar changes in the climate. In the summer it may have spent time watching the fish in a pond and even attempted to catch them. In the winter, however, frosts may cause the pond to ice up, and there is a possibility that the cat could fall into the freezing water, with dire consequences if it cannot escape. You may want to consider placing a net over the pond at this time of year as a safety precaution, anchoring it firmly in place with blocks around the edge.

This is also the time of year when antifreeze is added to car radiators. You must make sure that none is left accessible to cats in a garage, for they find this chemical very attractive and will drink it, with terrible results. The active constituent, ethylene glycol, is transformed to oxalic acid in the cat's body, and crystals are deposited in the kidneys, resulting in renal failure. There is little that can be done in such cases, because the damage to the cat's kidneys is irreversible.

Other chemicals, especially rat and mouse poisons, can pose a danger to cats. Warfarin, for example, results in anemia and internal hemorrhaging, and the cat often ingests a toxic dose by catching and eating rodents affected

CATS AND CHRISTMAS

The climbing abilities of cats can also make them vulnerable to poisons – for example, they may eat mistletoe (*Viscum album*) berries at Christmas, with serious consequences, climbing over furniture to get to the berries. Particularly close supervision of a cat is essential at this time of year, because it can end up injuring itself in various ways. Playing with the glass ornaments on a Christmas tree can result in a cut paw. If possible, use plastic decorations, so that, if your cat does climb up and knock them off the tree, it is unlikely to hurt itself badly. Similarly, make sure that the tree is adequately supported, because some kittens find this an irresistible climbing challenge and may topple the tree as a result. Try to avoid purchasing a tree whose needles fall rapidly, because there is a risk that these could penetrate your cat's paws, like a splinter, and cause considerable pain. The cat will appear lame and will be reluctant for you to examine its foot. Almost certainly it will have to be sedated by your veterinarian to enable the source of the irritation to be tracked down and removed, before it moves higher up the leg. If you have a Christmas tree growing in a pot, make sure you cover over the soil with gravel, or you may find that the cat uses this as a substitute for its litter box.

BELOW: Cats will poison themselves by drinking antifreeze.

ABOVE, (left & right): The appearance of your cat may change somewhat through the year. In the summer, it may have a relatively thin coat. At the start of winter, some cats gain a denser underfur, to protect against the cold, and may also develop a distinctive ruff of fur around the neck, although this depends to some extent on the breed or individual. This change is far less marked in short-haired cats.

by the poison, which accumulates in the body. Treatment may be possible, but only if the symptoms are identified in time.

Cats are particularly vulnerable to picking up poisons as they wander around the neighborhood. They often end up with poison on their paws, which they then lick clean, inadvertently swallowing the chemical as a result. Corrosive poisons, such as diesel oil and kerosene, may damage the tissue of the mouth, causing blistering, while others can have more insidious effects.

If your cat suddenly collapses, has difficulty in breathing, or displays nervous symptoms, poisoning is always a possibility. You should seek help from your veterinarian without delay, because rapid treatment in such cases can make the difference between life and death. Even some household products which are generally assumed to be safe and beneficial, such as aspirin, can be deadly to cats. This is why it is so important not to attempt to treat any illness on your own but always to seek immediate veterinary advice.

CHOOSING A CATTERY

BELOW: A cutaway
illustration of a cattery,
showing the outside run, and
the double-door entry system,
to prevent escapes. Once
inside, there are snug
sleeping quarters for the cat,
along with a heat lamp if the
weather is very cold.

If you are going away at Christmas or during
the busy summer months, you may need to find
a cattery able to care for your pet while you are
on vacation. Try to arrange this as early as
possible, because, at peak periods, it can be
difficult to obtain a last-minute vacancy.
Satisfied customers tend to use the same
cattery each year and this obviously limits the

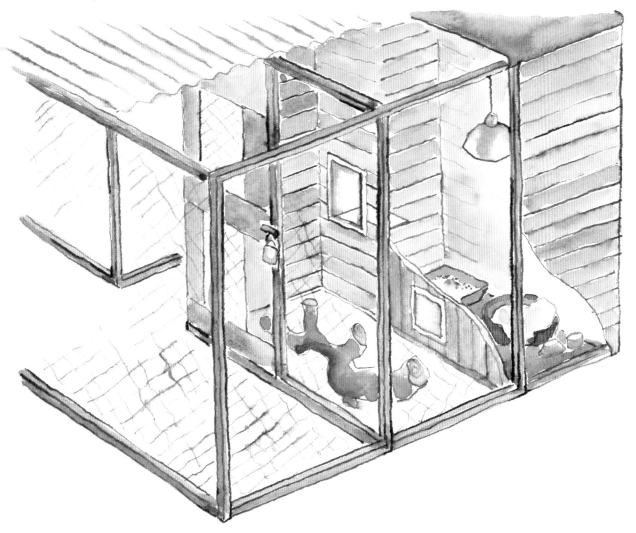

available space. You may be able to obtain a recommendation from a friend, but when you are considering boarding your cat for the first time, it is a good idea to arrange to visit the cattery before finalizing the arrangements. You can then be certain that you will feel happy leaving your pet there.

The state of the pens will give you an indication of the premises. They should be clean and secure, with no patched areas of mesh. A double-door entry system to prevent cats escaping is important and each cat should be housed on its own. An individual pen is vital, because cats often dislike being moved to a cattery and will resent the company of another cat in their quarters, even if they do not actually fight, therefore adding to the stress of the experience.

All reputable catteries will expect to see proof that your cat has received the necessary inoculations, and you will need to show the vaccination certificate completed by your vet for this purpose. If you have lost this, your vet should be able to provide you with a covering letter from the practice records, although you may have to pay an additional fee for this.

Find out from the cattery whether they want you to provide any bedding. This can help to settle a cat in unfamiliar surroundings, along with a favorite toy. When you leave your cat, it is also worth informing the cattery in writing of a contact telephone number for you while you are away, together with the name and address of your veterinarian, in case any problems arise in your absence. This is, of course, unlikely, but a worthwhile precaution. You may also want to tell them which brand of food your cat prefers, just in case it refuses to eat. This can be a problem with some cats, and a bowl of their favorite food may help to rekindle their appetite.

On the night before you go away, make sure you keep your cat inside. Cats sometimes apparently sense the fact that things are different, and they may disappear, ruining the start of your vacation, particularly if you are due to catch a plane. It may actually be better to book your cat into the cattery on the previous day to avoid any last-minute panics of this kind.

You may be asked to pay a deposit when you leave your cat. This is because there are

ABOVE: An outdoor cattery will give your kitten the opportunity to explore outside in safety, even in an urban area where there is likely to be heavy traffic. But wait until the weather is warm before placing your kitten here, and provide a snug sleeping area as well.

sometimes unscrupulous owners who dump their cats on an unsuspecting cattery, giving a false name and address, who then never return to collect their pet. Provided that you obtain a receipt for any payment made, there should be no problem over this type of arrangement. If you suspect that you may be delayed on your return journey, inform the cattery in advance, and take their phone or fax number with you so that you can confirm the situation as soon as you can.

YOU
AND YOUR
CAT

*ABOVE: Regular veterinary
checkups will detect signs of
illness at an early stage.*

Advances in health care mean that cats have a long life expectancy, but they still remain as susceptible as ever to illnesses if they are not vaccinated against them. Young kittens must be protected against cat flu, which, in spite of its name, is not caused by a single virus. It can result from infection, by either feline viral rhinotracheitis (FVR) virus or feline calicivirus (FCV).

ABOVE: Kittens can be infected by their mother before birth, via their placental connection or when suckling.

Signs of FVR infection are fairly consistent. The cat develops severe sneezing, coughing, and salivation, as well as a loss of appetite and a raised temperature. The symptoms of FCV may vary from cat to cat, depending on the strain of the virus, but it generally causes a less severe illness. Ulceration of the tongue is a fairly consistent feature, but discharges from the nose are not so apparent. There is always a risk of a secondary bacterial infection,

BELOW: Sneezing is another way in which viral infections can be spread.

RIGHT: Food can expose a kitten to both bacterial and parasitic illnesses.

however, and these infections sometimes become chronic, so that a kitten infected early in life may develop long-standing sinusitis.

There are vaccines to protect against both these conditions, and they are generally given together with a vaccine against feline infectious enteritis (FIE), also known as feline panleukopenia (FPL). This is a parvovirus infection, which spreads easily and can

BELOW: Wounds should always be treated, to prevent a localised infection, which could become more serious.

sometimes result in sudden death in susceptible cats. A sharply raised temperature, coupled with diarrhea, which is often stained with blood, are the typical symptoms. Dehydration rapidly follows, and death usually occurs within five days.

Any cats that do recover from FIE are liable to suffer from episodes of diarrhea throughout their lives because of damage to the intestinal lining. This virus can also be transmitted across the placenta during pregnancy, and it typically damages the nervous system of the kittens. Pregnant cats should never receive a live vaccine, because this may trigger an identical reaction.

The benefits of vaccination are, however, clear-cut, and a killed vaccine is safe for all healthy cats. Your vet will be able to advise you on the type most suitable for your kitten. A typical vaccination schedule will be for the first injection to be given at nine weeks of age, followed by the second after an interval of three weeks. Annual boosters will subsequently be required.

FELINE IMMUNOLOGY

———∞———

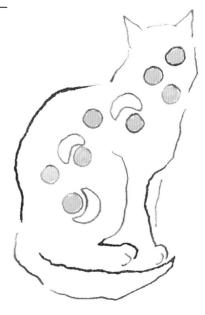

ABOVE: Foreign bodies, bacteria, or viruses enter the cat's body, usually through areas such as the nose and the intestines.

ABOVE: Antibodies are produced in these areas, and in the bloodstream by white blood cells (lymphocytes).

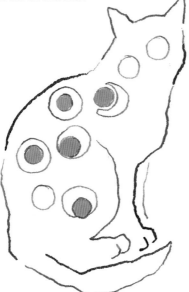

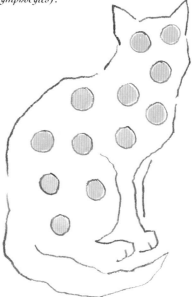

ABOVE: The antibodies attach themselves to the bacteria in order to neutralize them.

ABOVE: Once neutralized, the bacteria are fully engulfed by other white blood cells (macrophages).

It is also possible to protect against another common cause of respiratory disease, resulting from infection by *Chlamydia psittaci.* This can be given at the same time as the previous vaccines, but be guided by your veterinarian. You will also need to discuss the possibility of a Feline Leukemia Virus (FeLV) vaccination. Although the vaccine may not necessarily be as effective as those mentioned previously, it still conveys a high degree of protection against what can be a fatal disease. Cats living in close proximity to each other in towns are most at risk of contracting this infection. Blood testing should help to confirm that your cat is free of this chronic disease, which affects the immune system.

In many parts of the world, including North America, the dreaded viral illness known as rabies is still present within the wildlife population, and it can be spread to domestic cats if they are bitten by an infective animal, such as a fox or squirrel. The virus will then develop in the cat's body, taking as long as four months to manifest itself, because the virus tracks slowly up the peripheral nervous system and the effects will not become obvious until it reaches the central nervous system.

Cats suffering from clinical rabies are aggressive and exceedingly dangerous because of the threat they pose to people. A bite from an infected cat is likely to spread the illness to the person concerned, as the virus is present in the cat's saliva. After a period of as long as four days in this state, the cat starts to become paralyzed and dies soon afterward. Unlike humans, cats display no signs of hydrophobia – fear of water – when suffering from the terminal stages of rabies.

Thankfully, there is an effective vaccine to protect your kitten from this fatal disease, and in some parts of the USA, for example, it is a legal requirement for cats to be vaccinated in areas where rabies is present. This is, in any event, an essential measure.

RABIES

Rabies is a viral infection, usually transmitted to a cat as the result of a bite from another rabid animal. Only certain parts of the world, notably islands such as Great Britain, Hawaii, Ireland, Iceland, and Australia are free of this disease. It is a serious illness, being a zoonotic disease – one that can be transmitted from animals to people – and, in this particular case, it is almost inevitably fatal.

The risk posed by rabies, at least in Europe, may be less of a threat in the future, however, with the advent of new vaccines. The idea is to bait high-risk areas with the vaccine, so that foxes, which are the major wildlife reservoir for the disease here, will become immune and therefore widespread immunity will develop. As a result, the overall incidence of infection declines, and so does the risk to cats, and therefore people as well.

Rabies has a variable incubation period, which is influenced mainly by the place of the bite. If this is low down on the limb, the virus will take longer – perhaps several months – to track up the peripheral nerves to the central nervous system, resulting in clinical signs of illness. However, if the bite is in the vicinity of the neck, symptoms may well be apparent in weeks. Early indications of rabies may be a change of tone in the cat's voice, followed by uncontrolled aggression, with infectious saliva actually drooling from the mouth by this stage. The cat will start convulsing, and may then become comatose, before death finally occurs.

It is not necessary to get bitten to develop rabies. Open cuts on the hand can be equally dangerous. If you suspect that you may have been exposed to the virus, wash the wound thoroughly with alcohol, or rinse thoroughly, and seek medical attention without delay.

P A R A S I T I C P R O B L E M S

Even the best-cared-for cats can catch fleas,
and, with more homes than ever having central
heating, fleas have become a potential problem
throughout the year. Regular grooming will
alert you to their presence at an early stage,
before they reach plague proportions, and you
may see traces of flea dirt among loose hairs in
the comb. These take the form of minute black
specks, which, if placed on white paper and
splashed with water, will dissolve into reddish
deposits. This is undigested blood, on which
fleas feed directly through the cat's skin.

Fleas can transmit disease by this means, as
well as causing intense irritation, because their
saliva is injected into the cat's body when they

*BELOW: Two cats meeting
may result in the
transference of fleas from one
to the other.*

L I F E - C Y C L E   O F   T H E   F L E A

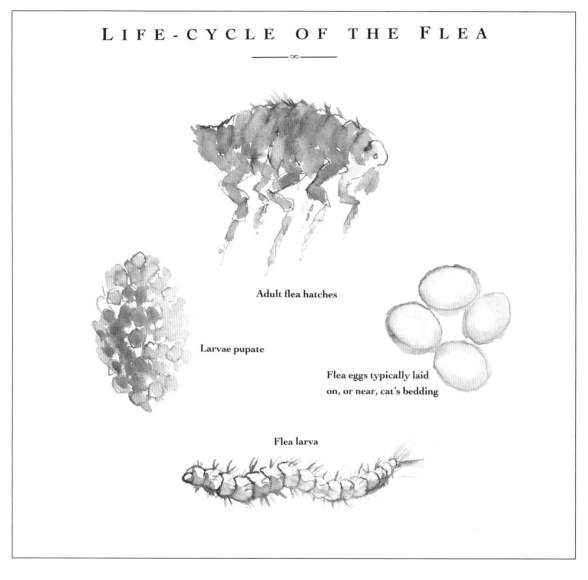

Adult flea hatches

Larvae pupate

**Flea eggs typically laid
on, or near, cat's bedding**

Flea larva

feed. In time, a cat can become sensitized to components in the saliva, and this results in an allergic reaction, which can be severe. Cat fleas can also be transmitted to dogs in the house, and they may also bite people, although they will not live on humans.

The life cycle of the flea is such that a single female can give rise to thousands of offspring within weeks, and it is therefore essential that they are controlled at the earliest possible opportunity. It is possible to treat a kitten with either a powder or a spray, but take particular care to read the manufacturer's instructions. Not all such products are suitable for young cats, and preparations that are intended for use with dogs may not be safe for cats of any age. You will also need to use such products carefully, particularly if you keep fish. Such chemicals are likely to be deadly to them, should they contaminate a pond, for example.

E L I Z A B E T H A N C O L L A R

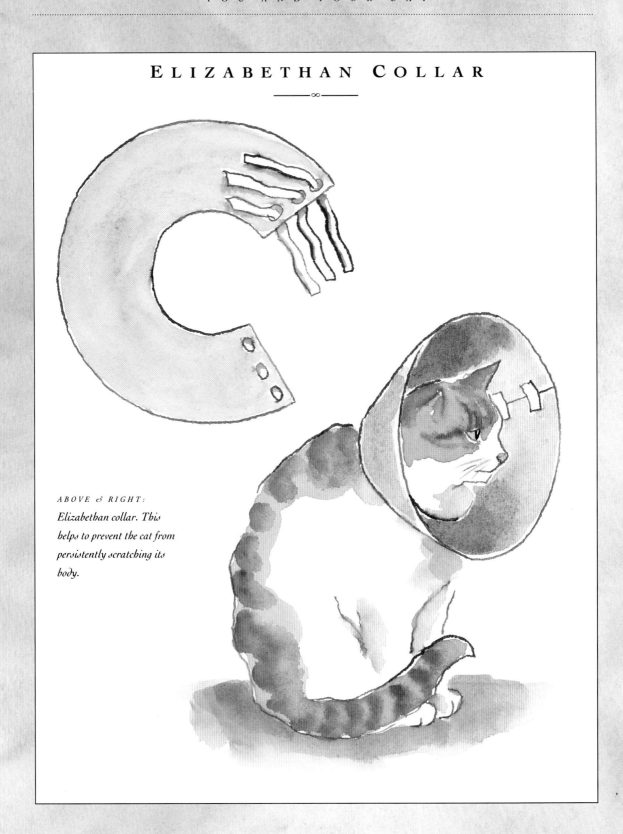

ABOVE & RIGHT:

*Elizabethan collar. This
helps to prevent the cat from
persistently scratching its
body.*

If your kitten has a severe infestation of fleas or lice, you may need to wash it in a special medicated shampoo. Lice are sometimes seen on young cats, but they rarely present a problem, because they spend their entire lives on the cat, being passed by direct contact. Fleas, on the other hand, are much more mobile and will leap off and breed in or around the cat's bedding. It is, therefore, not sufficient just to treat the kitten – you will need to wash its bed and bedding thoroughly, and vacuum the carpets repeatedly, as the microscopic flea larvae are likely to be hiding there.

As a precautionary measure, you can obtain flea collars for cats, which contain either chemicals or natural ingredients that deter fleas. These need to be fitted carefully, however, so that there is no risk of the young cat becoming caught up by the collar, which could have fatal consequences. In some cases, contact with the skin can cause a local adverse reaction, while, of course, as a young kitten grows, the collar must be loosened accordingly. For these reasons, it is sometimes not recommended to fit a collar of this type to a cat under six months old.

A kitten suffering from fleas may also be likely to develop a *Dipylidium* tapeworm infestation in its gut. This is because of a remarkable association between these two groups of parasites. As the microscopic tapeworm eggs are passed out of the cat's body they may adhere to the fur around the anus. Here, they may be ingested by a flea larva and begin their development in the flea's body. Then, as the cat grooms itself, it may inadvertently swallow a parasitized flea. The immature tapeworm completes its development within the cat's body. It is, therefore, important to treat kittens for tapeworms regularly, particularly when they have fleas. Other types of tapeworms rely on a similar life cycle involving rodents.

Nematodes, or roundworms, can also pose a problem, especially for kittens, and a heavy infestation may result in a poor growth rate, diarrhea and a rather potbellied appearance. There are various types of these so-called ascarids, of which *Toxocara cati* is probably most significant. Like other similar worms, its eggs are passed out in the feces and, after a few days, these will be directly infective to cats. This parasite may also cycle through rodents, with the cat becoming infected from its prey, so hunting cats are particularly vulnerable to such worms.

In addition, not all *Toxocara cati* larvae develop at once, having migrated through the organs of the body, such as the lungs and heart. Some remain dormant in the tissues of female cats and are activated by pregnancy. They are then passed out in the queen's milk to

BELOW: Special flea comb. Narrow teeth locate fleas in the cat's coat.

her kittens, who are infested with the parasite almost immediately after birth.

You should discuss a deworming program with your veterinarian when you take the kitten for its first appointment. It is usual to treat kittens for ascarids every month, for the first six months, and to repeat the treatment about three times a year if the cat roams. The first treatment for tapeworms is given at the age of six months, and is repeated at intervals throughout the cat's life.

In some parts of the world, another type of parasitic worm may be of concern to cat-

owners. Heartworms (*Dirofilaria immitis*) are transmitted by insect bites, and they are a particular problem in eastern and central areas of the USA, as well as in southern Europe and Australia. Regular medication may be advisable, because these worms can multiply in the circulatory system and ultimately block the arteries to the heart, causing collapse and sudden death.

Hookworm is another feline parasite found in the warmer parts of the world. The *Ancylostoma* worms can be a serious threat, causing anemia in kittens. In some cases, it is

BELOW: Vaccination is helping to control the major viral illnesses, with research to produce further vaccines also continuing.

GIVING A TABLET TO A CAT

RIGHT: Hold the head up as shown, and pry the lower jaw downward, dropping the pill as far as possible down in the direction of the back of the throat.

RIGHT: Finally, close the jaws and keep them closed. This will encourage the cat to swallow the pill.

possible that the larvae can penetrate directly through the skin, and eggs are passed out in the feces.

The signs of some parasitic worms may be quite specific. If they are infested with the feline lungworm (*Aelurostrongylus abstrusus*), which is particularly common in western Scotland, as well as occurring in the USA and Australia, cats will cough repeatedly, particularly after a period of exercise, and this leads to loss of condition. The adult lungworms inhabit the respiratory tract, and this is where they release their eggs. The larvae are coughed up and then pass through the cat's digestive tract, before undergoing an amazing two-staged process of development. First, the larvae must be eaten by a slug or snail, and then, in turn, the mollusk has to be consumed by a rodent, which acquires the infective, immature lungworm. Finally, cats become infected by eating a rodent which is carrying the parasite.

Hunting prey of this type or eating raw meat also renders cats susceptible to the protozoan parasite known as *Toxoplasma gondii.* This is an organism, which generally gives rise to few symptoms, with about 1 percent of all cats in the USA thought to be infected by this parasite. Control is achieved by preventing a cat gaining access to the infection.

G I V I N G   L I Q U I D   M E D I C I N E   T O   A   C A T

LEFT: A syringe will make this easier, but you will probably want someone to hold the cat so that you will not be scratched. Slowly dribble the medicine in at the side of the mouth, so as not to choke the cat.

Concern about this parasite centers on its possible effect on pregnant women, who can acquire the infection from contact with cat feces. Wearing gloves, both when changing the litter box and when gardening is to be recommended. It is possible for a medical test to be carried out to see if you already have antibodies to the infection, and many people who have had previous contact with cats will already possess antibodies. If a woman has not been exposed previously, however, there is a risk that an infection during pregnancy could harm her developing child by crossing the placenta, and might lead to miscarriage. The illness itself is known as toxoplasmosis.

RIGHT: If you use a spoon, the jaws will need to be pried apart, so you can tip the medicine slowly into the cat's mouth. It is almost inevitable that some will get spilled using this method.

T Y P I C A L   T A P E W O R M
L I F E   C Y C L E
———— ∞ ————

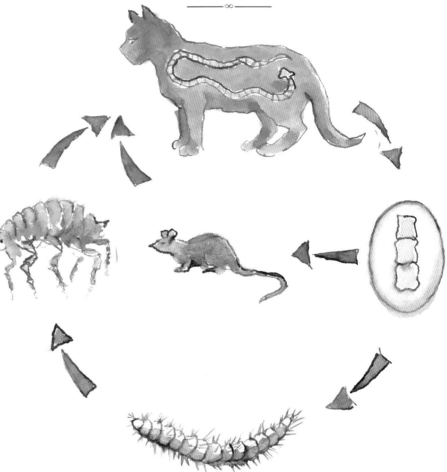

RIGHT: Tapeworm segments called proglottids, full of eggs, pass out of cat's body. The eggs may then be eaten by flea larvae or mice, and begin their development here. Subsequently, if a cat swallows an infected flea or mouse, then it is likely to develop a tapeworm infection. This is an example of an indirect life cycle, since an intermediate host is required to spread the infection. Cats cannot infect themselves directly.

R I N G W O R M
———— ∞ ————

In spite of its name, ringworm is not a parasitic disease, but is caused by a fungus. Symptoms in cats are relatively mild – you may notice some broken hair, in a circular pattern.

The problem with ringworm is that it is also a zoonosis – that is, it is a disease that can be transmitted from cats to people. It causes red, circular patches, typically on the skin of the forearms where the skin is in contact with the cat's fur when it is picked up. It may be possible for your veterinarian to diagnose ringworm on your cat by means of a piece of equipment called a Wood's Lamp, which causes the fungus to fluoresce as a bright, apple-green area, but in some cases, culturing may be required. Treatment with specific antibiotics for cats and people is possible, but will be protracted, lasting for at least a month.

TYPICAL ROUNDWORM
LIFE CYCLE

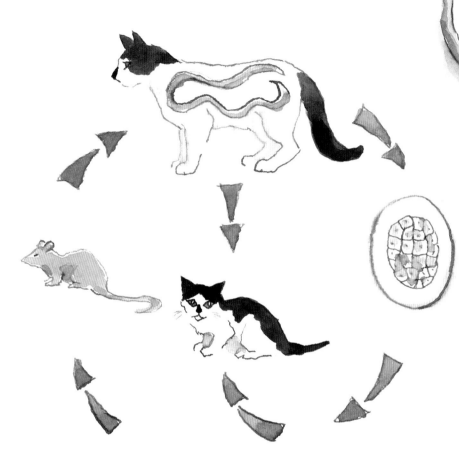

LEFT: Roundworm develops in cat's intestines. Eggs passed out of the body spend a short time in the environment, and then are infective for other cats as well as rodents. Kittens may be infected before birth from their mother, and they can also acquire roundworms by eating rodents carrying the parasite.

TICKS

These parasites are most unlikely to affect a kitten until it wanders outside. Ticks tend to attach themselves to grazing animals, but will parasitize cats on occasions, especially in sheep-farming areas. Sucking blood, ticks are also capable of spreading diseases. As they feed, they swell up in size, remaining anchored in the skin by their mouthparts.

You are most likely to discover them when grooming your kitten, and, although it may be tempting to pull them off, this is not recommended, as it is likely to lead to a local infection. It is much better to coat the tick in petroleum jelly, which will block its breathing pore and cause it to release its grip in due course without problems.

S I G N S   O F   P O S S I B L E   I L L N E S S

It can be more difficult to detect problems in a young cat that goes out regularly. You may be uncertain whether it is suffering from diarrhea or whether it is constipated. You will be able to note its appetite, but even then, appearances can be deceptive. Your cat may appear to have lost its appetite because it is obtaining food elsewhere, through a neighbor's cat flap, for example.

Cats are generally remarkably healthy animals, but you should keep as close a check as possible on your pet. Early recognition of the symptoms of illness should, hopefully, lead to a more swift recovery. Watch for a hunched appearance, for example, if you see the cat urinating in the garden. This is likely to be indicative of a urinary tract problem, especially feline urological syndrome (FUS). There may be a total blockage in the urethra, and you should always seek veterinary attention if this condition is suspected.

Another clear sign that all is not well with a kitten will be the appearance of the so-called "third eyelid" or "haws" (nictating membrane), which extends from the corner of the eyes near the nose and partially obscures the surface of the eyes themselves. This may be linked with more obvious symptoms, such as a discharge from the eyes or nose.

It may be useful to take your kitten's temperature, with a mercury thermometer. The bulb should be slid a short distance into the rectum, having been dabbed with a suitable lubricant. A cat's temperature should be approximately 101.5°F, although this can be slightly higher in a young kitten without necessarily giving you cause for concern.

LEFT: If the cat is choking, it may have swallowed a bone, and this must be removed at once. Open the jaws carefully and then gently try to pry the obstruction out of the mouth.

EYES

LEFT: If the third eyelid or nictating membrane is evident extending across the eyes, it is a sign of poor health.

LEFT: The eyes can be wiped with cotton balls to keep them clean.

ABOVE: A dropper may be useful to give eyedrops. Try to make your cat does not struggle or blink at the critical moment, causing the medication to miss its target.

FELINE UROLOGICAL SYNDROME

LEFT: A cat will normally crouch, as shown, with a straight back when urinating. If it appears hunched up (below) this is a possible indication of feline urological syndrome, a serious condition which causes a partial, or even total, blockage of the flow of urine out of the body from the bladder.

EARS

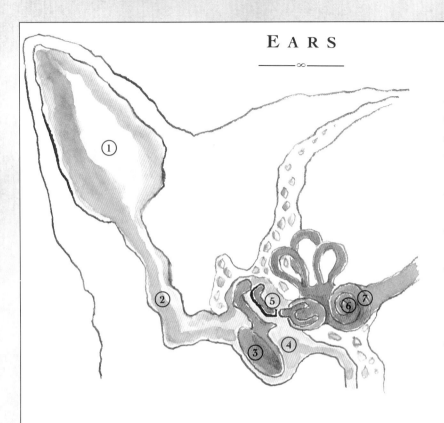

LEFT: The pinna *(1) acts as a funnel, channeling the sound waves down the* external auditory canal *(2) to the* eardrum *(3). In the* middle ear *(4), the* ossicles *(5) act as a system of levers which convert the weaker vibrations of the eardrum into the stronger vibrations of the oval window, part of the* cochlea *(6). This then sends nerve signals along the* auditory nerve *(7) to the brain.*

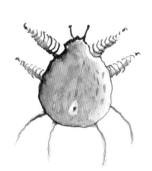

LEFT & RIGHT: Ear *mites can be a problem, and can cause severe irritation in the ear, along with bacteria and fungi. Inflammation of the ear is likely to result.*

RIGHT: This causes the cat *to scratch repeatedly, in an attempt to lessen the irritation. Prompt veterinary treatment will be required under these circumstances, with a buildup of brown wax in the ear canal being visible.*

If you are at all worried about your kitten's health, contact your veterinarian without delay. Almost certainly, you will need to take the kitten there for a visit so that it can have a proper examination, before a diagnosis is made and appropriate treatment given.

You may be asked to take a urine sample with you. This is not as difficult to obtain as you may fear, provided that the kitten remains confined indoors with a litter box. You may be able to persuade it to urinate in its box onto a plastic liner, without any litter. The tray can then be taken outside and the urine tipped carefully into a suitable container. Do not use a container that may have held sugary items, such as jelly, because lingering deposits in the jar will interfere with the test results. Only a relatively small volume of urine will be necessary, in any case, so a large container is not required.

Provided that your kitten is well cared for, in a secure environment, and receives its inoculations regularly, you and your family should enjoy many years of pleasure with your new pet. Cats show few obvious external signs of aging, and they can remain playful well into their teens, making them excellent company for young and old alike.

I N D E X

PICTURE CREDITS

Quintet Publishing would like to thank the
following for supplying photographs for
this book.
Animal Photography pages 16, 20, 33, 44
Jacana, Berthoule Hervé page 11
Marc Henrie pages 2, 9, 15, 19, 21, 22, 23, 24,
25, 26, 27, 28, 29, 30, 31, 39, 50, 56, 68, 71, 84,
89, 95